THE MENTAL HEALTH PROFESSIONAL AND THE LEGAL SYSTEM

Report No. 131

THE MENTAL HEALTH PROFESSIONAL AND THE LEGAL SYSTEM

Formulated by the Committee on Psychiatry and Law

GROUP FOR THE ADVANCEMENT OF PSYCHIATRY

Published by

American Psychiatric Press, Inc.

Washington, DC
London, England

Manufactured in the United States of America on acid-free paper.
American Psychiatric Press edition published 1992.
1400 K Street, N.W., Washington, DC 20005
95 94 93 92 4 3 2 1

Library of Congress Cataloging-in-Publication Data

The Mental health professional and the legal system/formulated by the Committee on Psychiatry and Law, Group for the Advancement of Psychiatry.
p. cm.
Originally published: New York: Brunner/Mazel, c1991, in series: Report (Group for the Advancement of Psychiatry: 1984); no. 131.
Includes bibliographical references.
ISBN 0-87318-625-7 (pbk.).
1. Evidence, Expert—United States. 2. Forensic psychiatry—United States. 3. Insanity—Jurisprudence—United States. 4. Mental health personnel—Legal status, laws, etc.—United States. I. Group for the Advancement of Psychiatry. Committee on Psychiatry and Law.
[DNLM: 1. Expert Testimony. 2. Forensic Psychiatry—United States. W 740 M54851992a]
KF8965.M46 1992
347.73′67—dc20
[347.30767]
DNLM/DLC
for Library of Congress 92-7018
CIP

STATEMENT OF PURPOSE

The Group for the Advancement of Psychiatry has a membership of approximately 300 psychiatrists, most of whom are organized in the form of a number of working committees. These committees direct their efforts toward the study of various aspects of psychiatry and the application of this knowledge to the fields of mental health and human relations.

Collaboration with specialists in other disciplines has been and is one of GAP's working principles. Since the formation of GAP in 1946, its members have worked closely with such other specialists as anthropologists, biologists, economists, statisticians, educators, lawyers, nurses, psychologists, sociologists, social workers, and experts in mass communication, philosophy, and semantics. GAP envisages a continuing program of work according to the following aims:

1. To collect and appraise significant data in the fields of psychiatry, mental health, and human relations;
2. To reevaluate old concepts and to develop and test new ones;
3. To apply the knowledge thus obtained for the promotion of mental health and good human relations.

GAP is an independent group, and its reports represent the composite findings and opinions of its members only, guided by its many consultants.

The Mental Health Professional and the Legal System was formulated by the Committee on Psychiatry and Law. The members of this committee are listed on page vii. The members of the other GAP committees, as well as additional membership categories and current and past officers of GAP, are listed at the end of the report.

Committee on Psychiatry and Law
GROUP FOR THE ADVANCEMENT OF PSYCHIATRY

Jonas R. Rappeport, M.D., *Chairman*

Renee Binder, M.D.
J. Richard Ciccone, M.D.
Park E. Deitz, M.D., Ph.D.
John Donnelly, M.D.
Carl P. Malmquist, M.D.
Herbert C. Modlin, M.D.
Phillip J. Resnick, M.D.
Loren Roth, M.D.
Joseph Satten, M.D.
William Weitzel, M.D.
Howard Zonana, M.D.

Kurt Biehl, M.D., *Ginsburg Fellow*
Gregory E. Gray, M.D., *Ginsburg Fellow*
Bonnie T. Zima, M.D., *Ginsburg Fellow*

Lansing Crane, J.D., *Ittleson Consultant*

CONTENTS

THE MENTAL HEALTH PROFESSIONAL AND THE LEGAL SYSTEM

INTRODUCTION

Many mental health professionals fear involvement with and become unduly anxious when asked to become involved with the legal system. In part, this reticence is the result of insufficient understanding of the intricacies of that system. In the belief that knowledge reduces fear, the GAP Committee on Psychiatry and Law has developed this guide to the role of the mental health professional in the conduct of legal proceedings.

In this report, the role of the therapist in relation to the law in a matter involving a patient under treatment has been separated distinctly from that of the expert who is retained specifically to assist with a particular legal issue. In the classical therapeutic role, the therapist is the patient's or client's agent; in the expert-consultant role, the mental health professional may be the agent of either the attorney or the court. These differences may cause confusion at first, but, once understood, can both relieve anxiety and prevent harm. The mental health professional can function in many different ways in relation to the legal system: as a therapist, as an evaluator, as an expert witness, or as a consultant to an attorney or the court. Each role offers advantages and pitfalls for both the professional and the patient. We have tried to point out the most obvious and important problems that might be encountered.

Although authored primarily by psychiatrists, we have written this guide for all mental health professionals: psychiatrists, psychologists, social workers, psychiatric nurses, mental health counselors, and others. Thus, instead of referring to one particular profession, we use the terms "therapist," "expert," "expert witness," and "mental health professional" interchangeably. Similarly, we do not distinguish between "patient" and "client," and employ the term "patient" to refer to either.

The principles discussed here are relevant to all mental health professionals. We have not discussed in detail psychological tests and their uses. In a similar vein, we have not focused on the particular roles of the psychologist and social worker in the courtroom. To have included more detail on both of these important contributions to forensic work was beyond our objective to create a brief, limited, and concise guide; there are several excellent texts on forensic psychology and social work practice. We also have not discussed those special issues that arise when the law deals with children and adolescents; these also are considered in special texts.

On the first reading, you may wish to review the entire text. Later, the volume should become a reference guide, used in part or as a whole as needed. The GAP Committee on Psychiatry and Law hopes that you will find this guide helpful in clearing a path through the wilderness of the law.

I
OVERVIEW

1

YOU AND THE LAW

Involvement by mental health professionals with the legal system is an increasingly common occurrence that, with knowledge and preparation, may become a challenging and enjoyable experience. Contact with the legal system may be either as a therapist or as a consulting expert. The roles differ widely, but, in each case, the mental health professional is asked to answer or to help others answer questions for legal ends.

In the legal arena, questions are constructed in specific legal language, and the mental health professional must attempt to communicate in the same language, translating scientific knowledge and terminology to the rubric of the legal profession. The professional thus presents a medical/legal opinion written in language that can be understood clearly by both the legal profession and the lay person. Pollack (1971) describes the mental health practitioner in the forensic role as a tactician, a logician, and a clinician.

What Pollack does not suggest is that in the forensic role, the therapist is also a tightrope walker—balancing between the rights and obligations of the therapist-patient relationship and those of the legal system. Issues at the interface of the clinical and legal systems, such as confidentiality, patients' rights, duty to warn, and commitment, among others, raise conflicts and questions for the therapist when faced with a patient in treatment and the same patient in court.

This volume provides a road map through the legal wilderness for the mental health professional who sometimes must serve the patient and the legal system. Prepared by experienced forensic psychiatrists, it is not intended as a textbook, but rather as a guide to this medicolegal interface. The authors, who have participated frequently in the legal system, bring a total of over 200 years of experience to this volume. This volume is not intended, however, as a substitute for consultation with either forensic experts or personal counsel when faced with a legal question. It is designed to allay fears and concerns about the legal experience, to educate about the process and content of legal issues in mental illness, and ultimately to help make the clinician's experience with the legal system satisfying.

Part I provides a basic understanding of the legal language, content, and process, and the ways in which the legal system and mental health treatment systems intersect. Part II describes the roles and responsibilities of the therapist whose patient becomes party to a legal dispute. This part also provides an overview of civil commitment and the legal process with which the mental health professional is most frequently faced. Part III details the function of the evaluating mental health expert, providing a step-by-step description of the requisites of this role. Appendices include a glossary of legal terms, a competency assessment instrument, a guide for the evaluation of permanent mental health impairments (occupational health), and the ethical guidelines of the American Academy of Psychiatry and the Law. For those who may be considering a career in forensic psychiatry, the appendix also contains information about forensic education and career options. References and a bibliography provide guidance for further independent review of the subject.

REFERENCE

Pollack, S. (1971). Principles of forensic psychiatry for psychiatric-legal opinion making in 1971. In C. Wecht (Ed.), *Legal-medical annual*, (pp. 270–271). New York: Appleton-Century-Crofts.

2

THE LAW AND THE LEGAL PROCESS

The mental health professional choosing to engage in forensic work will encounter a system of goals, assumptions, and methods distinctly different from those found in the clinical setting. The legal system defines and enforces rights and responsibilities, focusing on the establishment of generic values and regulating human conduct. Moreover, "the law" is a collection of defined rights and responsibilities with a foundation in many sources. For example, when a court defines "due process of law" to include the right of a criminal defendant to the assistance of a mental health practitioner in developing his or her legal defense, it adds to our body of constitutional law. Similarly, legislative enactment of a statute prohibiting the claim of an insanity defense by defendants who are voluntarily intoxicated at the time of a crime also defines the law. The processes and procedures through which federal and state law is applied are based on an adversarial system. The mental health professional who serves as a witness must have a fundamental understanding of both the origins of the law and how the law is applied in practice to a specific problem.

SOURCES OF THE LAW

In the US, there are four primary sources of law: the constitution, the courts, the legislature, and administrative agencies. The federal Constitution and its state analogues have established and delegated law-making powers to federal judiciary, legislative, and executive branches. Amendments to the federal Constitution delineate the boundaries circumscribing the exercise of state and federal powers, with the first ten amendments—the Bill of Rights—expressly limiting the powers of the federal government. The Fourteenth Amendment prohibits states from denying their citizens either due process of law or equal protection of the law.

The hierarchical character of our legal process is reflected by the sixth Article of the federal Constitution:

> This constitution and the laws of the United States which shall be made in pursuance thereof . . . shall be the supreme law of the land and the judges in every state shall be bound thereby, anything in the constitution or laws of any state to the contrary notwithstanding.

Known as the Supremacy Clause, Article 6 establishes that all laws—statutes, state constitutions, judicial decisions, local ordinance, and administrative rulings—must bow to the principles of the US Constitution.

While the Constitution was understood to have created three equal and separate branches of federal government, the Supreme Court—the judicial branch—has emerged as the final arbiter of the meaning of the Constitution. Thus, for the purposes of law-making, it has been elevated above both the legislature and the executive branch. While the executive branch and the legislature may codify law, the Court, through its interpretive powers, has the capacity to invalidate a law if the Court deems it to be unconstitutional.

This power to interpret the Constitution introduces the second major source of law: judicial decision. In the words of Justice Marshall in *Marbury v. Madison* (1803), "Judicial power is the power to declare the law of the land." Court decisions are made in the context of either criminal or civil dispute resolution. The judicial function requires the identification and application of appropriate law to the facts that are established at a trial, leading to a resolution of a dispute between two (or more) parties. Inevitably, the process involves interpretation, whether, for example, clarifying the meaning of dangerousness as incorporated in a commitment statute or the requirements of procedural due process. This exercise of the judicial function creates *case law*. In turn, established case law acts as a precedent for future courts to follow in similar situations. Over time, court actions create a body of *judicial law*, interpreting constitution, statute, and prior case law alike.

Common law is English case law, developed primarily by its courts' identification of widely shared principles and customs in order to resolve cases. These decisions then become precedent in the resolution of new cases. Common law is the purest form of judicial law and is the source of the principle of *stare decisis*, a concept expressing respect for precedent. Literally translated as "let the decision stand," *stare decisis* represents the supreme mandate to judges when interpreting law. Presumably, if at two different points of time, the exact same facts are presented in different legal disputes, the court's determination of the rights and responsibilities in the first case should control the resolution of the second dispute.

British common law was the law of the land at the time of our independence and is the source of most of our definitions of crime and our concept of criminal responsibility. It forms the basis for our concept of the insanity defense as well as for most of our forms of civil action—negligence, breach of contract, and such intentional torts as battery, defamation, and the like. However, historically, American courts have not articulated new common law in the same manner as English courts. Rather, our legal system relies on legislatures and administrative agencies to create new law, and expects American courts largely to confine their role to the interpretation of these laws. Since, however, the interpretive function is powerful, courts continue to be a primary source of American law.

Legislative lawmaking occurs in an arena wholly separate from the judicial process. Special interest groups, experts, and lobbyists petition legislatures for the creation of new law without regard to legal precedent. Generally, legislation is designed to regulate a broad area of social conduct, not to resolve a specific dispute between individuals, and all language contained in adopted legislation has the force of law. When reviewing legislation, therefore, it is essential to read the entire text, word for word, because each word, in effect, may create new law.

The *executive branch* of government carries out the governmental tasks embodied in statutes and establishes regulations and policies to that end. Those policies and regulations form the basis of the fourth source of the law—*administrative law*. For example, the licensing of a facility or a practitioner requires the establishment of qualifications and needed resources in light of a perceived standard of public welfare. To grant or withhold a license in specific circumstances is to make a legal determination and to create a precedent for the future. While the executive branch can adopt regulations or grant licenses with far less formality than is required for the legislative branch to adopt legislation or for the judicial branch to reach a court decision, the actions of the executive branch must be based on a statutory or Constitutional delegation of power and must be consistent from case to case. Courts are often asked to interpret the legality of administrative action in light of the powers granted by Congress or the Constitution, and will strike down administrative actions that violate this hierarchy of legal authority.

THE JUDICIAL PROCESS

The judicial process is a system of institutions and procedures designed to resolve legal disputes. Figure 1 illustrates the possible course of a criminal case from arrest through appeal to ultimate release. Figure 2 shows the analogous course of a civil proceeding in which a plaintiff is seeking compensation for personal injury.

The civil and criminal processes contain many similarities. Each begins with a statement of allegations (indictment or complaint) brought by the injured party (victim via the prosecutor or the plaintiff). The issues are narrowed by motions to delete charges, to define applicable law, and to exclude or to allow the discovery of certain evidence. A jury is chosen and asked to render an opinion on the truth of the factual arguments of the parties. Each side is given the opportunity both to present evidence of its perception of the truth and to test the

THE COURSE OF A CRIMINAL TRIAL

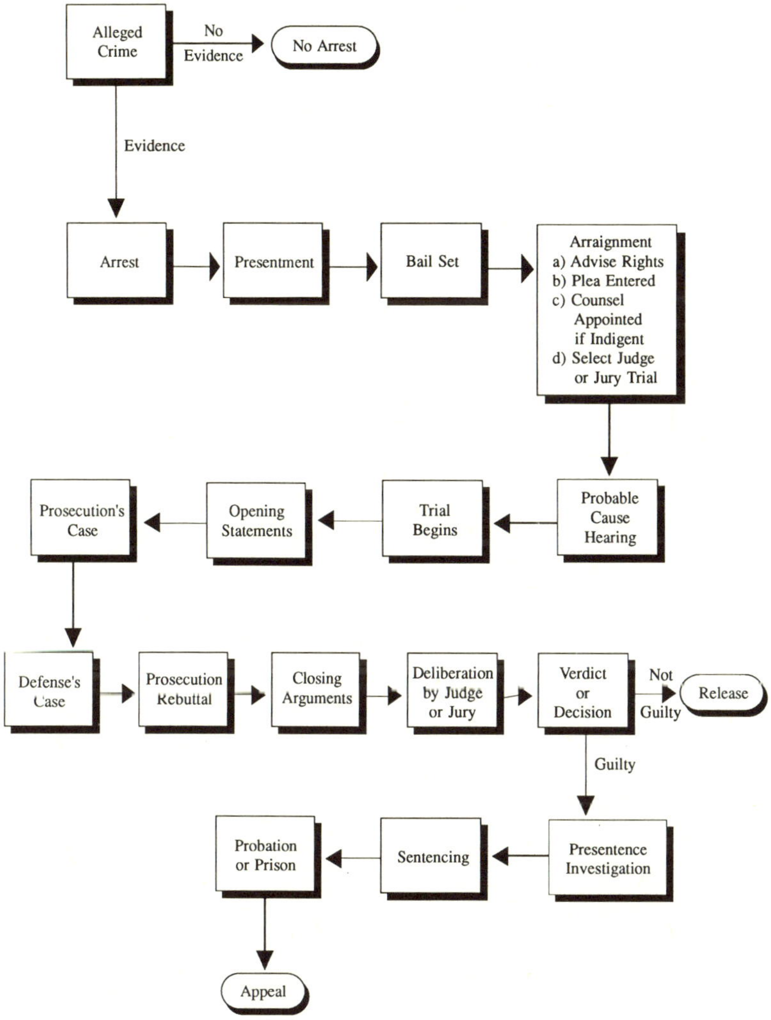

Figure 1

THE COURSE OF A CIVIL TRIAL

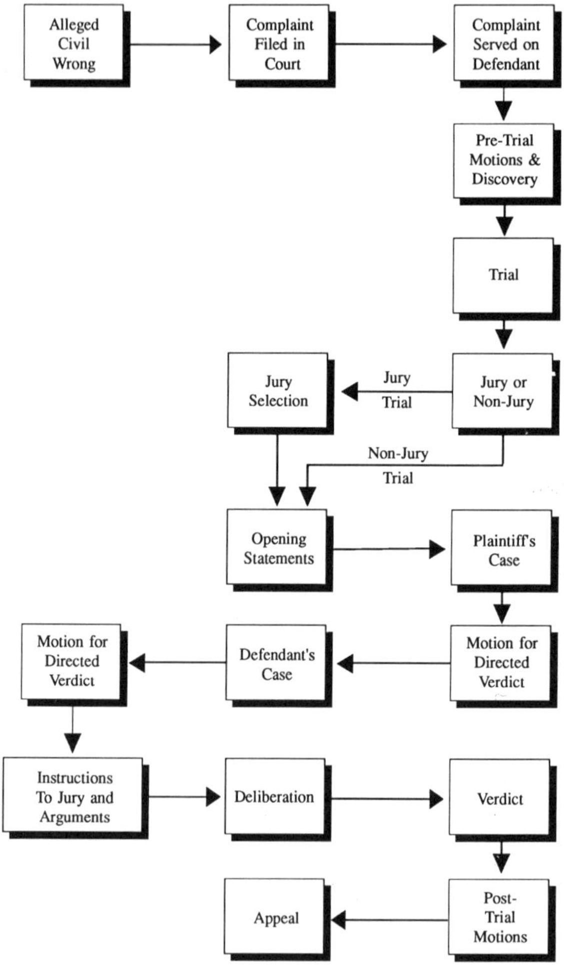

Figure 2

opponent's version by cross-examination. The judge determines the applicable law and tells the jury how to apply the law to its factual conclusions.

Central to the judicial process is the concept of the "burden of proof." In order to prevail in either a civil or criminal action, the plaintiff (or "moving party") is expected to satisfy a specific standard of persuasion. The standard reflects the value placed on the issues in controversy. In a criminal case in which human freedom is at stake, the moving party (the state) must be found to be overwhelmingly persuasive; it must prove its case "beyond a reasonable doubt." In civil actions in which monetary interests alone are in controversy, the moving party is held to a less stringent standard. In order to succeed, the party need only establish that, based on all the evidence, the factual propositions are more likely than not (a "preponderance of the evidence"). If a civil action involves more important social interests, such as civil commitment, in which personal liberty is at stake, factual allegations of the moving party often must be established by evidence that is "clear and convincing" to the fact finder(s).

Once the trial has been completed, the losing party may appeal to a higher court (Figure 3.). The higher or appellate court hears no new testimony and therefore does not reconsider the demeanor or credibility of witnesses. The appeals court only can decide whether to sustain or to reverse a verdict from below on the basis of legal and constitutional issues. For example, did the judge below render a proper explanation of the law to the jury? Did he admit or refuse to admit certain evidence in a proper manner, etc?

THE ADVERSARIAL PROCESS

The legal process is based on principles of advocacy and conflict that may be both alien and disturbing to many mental health professionals. Most cases involve a determination of facts long after the occurrence of the events in question. Trials reflect the belief that a determination of truth can best occur when the evidence offered is tested by those with an interest in

BASIC STRUCTURE OF UNITED STATES COURT SYSTEM

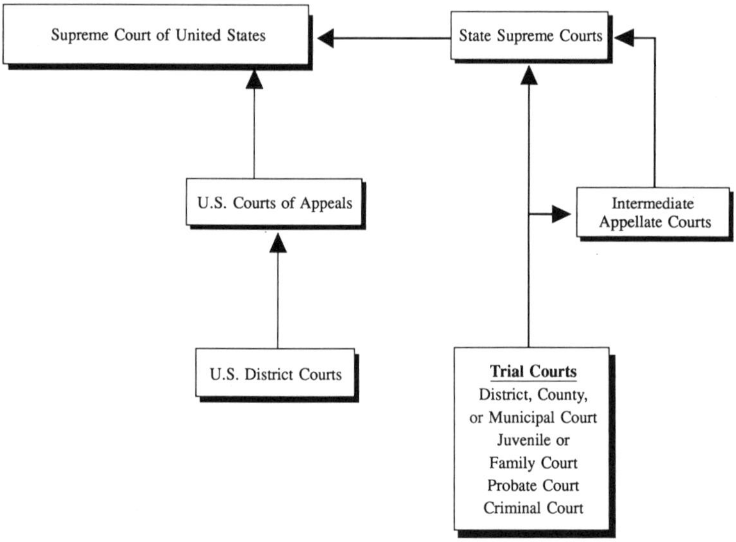

Figure 3

the outcome. This factual determination process is made even more adversarial by the advocacy roles accorded the parties. A fundamental precept of our legal process is that the truth will best be determined, and justice will most likely prevail, when competing viewpoints and interests are argued forcefully before an impartial fact finder, judge or jury, who then determines the "true" facts.

The American Bar Association's Code of Professional Responsibility includes the principle: "a lawyer should represent his client zealously within the bounds of the law" (American Bar Association, 1983). In its commentary on the Code, the ABA relates that principle to a lawyer's responsibility in the adversarial process:

> Our legal system provides for the adjudication of disputes governed by the rules of substantive, evidentiary, and procedural law. An adversary presentation counters the natural human tendency to judge too swiftly in terms of the familiar that which is not yet fully known; the advocate, by his zealous preparation and presentation of the facts and the law, enables the tribunal to come to the hearing with an open and neutral mind and to render impartial judgments. The duty of a lawyer to his client and his duty to the legal system are the same. (American Bar Association, 1983)

No feature of the legal process embodies the principles of conflict and advocacy more clearly than reliance on cross-examination as a tool in the search for truth. The rule against admitting "hearsay" (out-of-court statements) is largely founded on the belief that no evidence should be admitted if it cannot be tested by cross-examination. The constitutional right to confront witnesses embodies the same principle.

However, the techniques of cross-examination threaten mental health witnesses. Witnesses worry that they will appear foolish or make statements that are neither believable nor defensible. Yet, the properly prepared witness need not fear cross-examination, recognizing that it is the role of the adversarial system to test all data offered, whether it derives from the lay or the expert witness.

With a basic understanding of the nature of law and the legal process, much of the concern and even fear of involvement in legal proceedings on a patient's behalf may be allayed. Buttressed by an appropriate relationship with legal counsel representing the patient, the mental health professional, whether trained in forensics or not, can play a meaningful role in the judicial process. Involvement in the process represents both a right and a considerable responsibility. The next chapter describes the function of the mental health practitioner in the court, articulating a variety of questions to be asked and pitfalls to be avoided in engagement in the judicial process.

REFERENCES

American Bar Association. (1983). *Model rules of professional conduct—Canon 7*. Washington, DC: American Bar Association.
Marbury v. Madison, 5 U.S. 137 (1803).

3

THE NEED FOR MENTAL HEALTH PROFESSIONALS IN THE LEGAL SYSTEM

Courts often call upon the expertise of mental health professionals to aid in the resolution of specific civil and criminal questions that bear both on mental capacity and on the relationship between mental disorders and the ability to function adequately. Clinical evaluations are needed to assist courts in a variety of areas:

Criminal

1. Competence to stand trial
2. Insanity defense
3. Pre-sentence
4. Capital sentencing
5. Extreme emotional disturbance (murder)
6. Insanity acquittee's release
7. Competence to be executed
8. Competence to be a witness
9. Mentally disordered sexual offender

Civil

1. Malpractice
2. Child custody/abuse
3. Disabled physicians
4. Psychic harm
5. SSDI
6. Workers' Compensation
7. Testamentary capacity

8. Civil commitment
9. Conservatorship or guardianship
10. Return to work or school

While not exhaustive, this list illustrates the range of forensic evaluations that may be undertaken within either the criminal or civil sectors of the legal system. A more detailed description of the scope of the mental health professional's involvement in these legal issues is contained in Chapter 4.

DEFENDING AGAINST ROLE CONFLICTS

While a therapist may be called to appear as a factual witness on behalf of a patient being seen in treatment, the role in conducting an evaluation in any one of these areas generally is consultative rather than therapeutic. In the consultation model, the primary responsibility is to the court or the attorney requesting the evaluation, not to the individual under evaluation. Moreover, the consultant and the subject of the evaluation should not establish a therapist/patient relationship.

When the relationship becomes blurred or misunderstood, the consulting mental health professional is likely to be confused by possible "nontherapeutic" examination results. For example, it is not unusual for a consultant to feel that, from the therapeutic vantage point, it may be in an individual's interests to be released from confinement or to have custody of a child. However, an opposite conclusion may be warranted from the vantage point of either societal safety or a child's best interests. If the consultant is also the therapist, then role conflicts (double agentry) increase, pitting the duties and responsibilities as a therapist against the duties as a consultant to the attorney or the court. Unfortunately, because issues of "double agentry" do not arise as frequently in the therapeutic context. many clinicians fail to consider important questions before performing consultations:

For whom is the consulting therapist working?
What is the specific question being asked?

Is the question within the consulting therapist's area of expertise?

What are the legal rules governing confidentiality in the examination?

Has the criminal defendant (or civil case plaintiff) been adequately informed of both the purpose of the evaluation and how the collected data may be used?

Are there legal or ethical conflicts that would preclude an agreement to act as a consultant?

Considerable time and effort may be required to delineate the answers to these questions. The person to be evaluated usually is least able to explicate them, stating only "I need this evaluation so I can go back to work" or "the court sent me." For this reason, it is preferable to obtain a written request from the court, attorney, or institution requesting the examination which specifies the question to be addressed in the evaluation.

Often, as initially stated by a requesting attorney or court, the questions themselves will have to be clarified.

Is he crazy?

Just do a psychiatric evaluation.

Will he be dangerous in the future?

Global questions of this nature usually cannot be answered in the conduct of a clinical evaluation. Clarification of the question at the outset will save time and embarrassment. Indeed, the need for an evaluation may be obviated altogether, particularly if the legal question cannot be framed in a meaningful way.

Once it is agreed that an evaluation will be performed, the expert has an obligation to provide as complete and objective an examination as required to address the questions posed. One of the most troubling issues in forensic work is the matter of advocacy. The expert should present an unbiased opinion based on the review of available records and reports and on the evaluation. However, the pressures to lean one way or another are very strong, emanating from the retaining source, the examinee, the bias of materials furnished, and the natural instinct to please. While a true "professional" should be able to manage this tendency to please, the pressures exerted by some attorneys are particularly strong. An additional problem is raised by the nonpunitive, forgiving personal orientation shared by many mental health professionals. Moreover, the mental health professional, by training, tries to understand and explain all human behavior in a rational or organized, dynamic fashion. As far as the law is concerned, however, understanding is not the same as excusing; treatment is not a fair equivalent of punishment, whether the latter is imprisonment or the imposition of a monetary fine. These are difficult problems. Experience helps overcome the pitfalls, but does not ensure perfection.

A judge must order a competency evaluation if there is any question that the defendant might be incompetent to stand trial. A judge usually will order an evaluation by a mental health professional in a child custody case. Sometimes, the judge chooses the expert, sometimes the attorneys agree from a list of names supplied by the court. The court-appointed expert, however, does not have a role that insulates the expert from examination and cross-examination. Either side may challenge the expert's opinion. A court-appointed expert may appear more important by virtue of the court's appointment. If allowed, the attorney whose side is favored by the expert's opinion will attempt to emphasize that supposed advantage. Ideally, any *expert* opinion should be the same regardless of the employer.

DEFENSE-REQUESTED EVALUATIONS: CRIMINAL JUSTICE SYSTEM

When a defendant's attorney requests an evaluation of a client with whom the expert has had no prior contact, the expert functions as a consultant to the defense attorney—a part of the defense team, the confidentiality of whose communications may be under attorney-client privilege. Because various jurisdictions may view the attorney-client privilege differently, it is important to ask the attorney whether the evaluation is confidential. The nature of the confidentiality should then be made explicit to the defendant at the time of the initial interview. Certainly, anything the defendant tells the examiner may be discussed with the defense attorney. The expert cannot decide that certain parts of the examination are confidential.

There may be certain limitations to confidentiality. For example, in a few states, once the defendant enters an insanity plea, any expert who has performed an evaluation may be called by the State. In other circumstances, the attorney who retains the expert may not be compelled to use the consultant; the other side, then, may not have access to the expert. Sometimes, an attorney will agree to make the results of an evaluation available to the other side. Any limitations on the extent of confidentiality should be made very clear before the evaluation occurs so the defendant is aware and can give a fully informed consent. Under these circumstances, there is no obligation to perform the evaluation until or unless the expert finds the conditions agreeable and believes there are no conflicts of interest or ethical considerations that might preclude involvement.

The attorney may ask the expert about weaknesses in his or her own case as well as about weaknesses on the other side.* Since the attorney has the legal obligation to present the best possible case for the client, it is appropriate for the attorney to ask that a report not be filed should its presentation be of potential harm to the defendant. However, depending on the jurisdiction's rules, the other side may be able to call the expert as a witness.

In all ways, the expert who performs an evaluation on behalf of the defense becomes an integral part of the defense counsel's team. Careful consideration must be given to potential

---

*In a recent Supreme Court decision (*Ake v. Oklahoma*, 1985), the Court delineated a criminal defendant's right to a psychiatric evaluation to assist in the preparation of a defense at critical phases of the proceedings. In addition, the Court explicitly noted the attorney's need for assistance in cross-examination of opposing experts. If a consultant to the attorney has completed an objective evaluation and has formulated conclusions and opinions, it may be appropriate for that person to function in a consultative capacity by reviewing weaknesses of opposing experts' reports or testimony.

conflict of interest or ethical considerations before a therapist adopts this consultative, rather than therapeutic, role.

PROSECUTION-REQUESTED EVALUATIONS: CRIMINAL JUSTICE SYSTEM

Most of the same basic tenets that govern defense-requested evaluations—use of reports, confidentiality—also apply to prosecution requests for evaluation. When evaluating a defendant at the request of the prosecutor, the expert must be careful to give the defendant adequate warning that material gathered might be used by the State in its prosecution. The absence of confidentiality in the interview process must be made explicit to the defendant, a requirement not dissimilar to the Miranda warning given by the police. In the main, greater cautions arise here than are applicable to the defense expert or consultant.

In the adversarial system, the prosecution and the defense may each be privy to certain information that is not available to the other side. As a consultant to the prosecutor, it is important to keep such information confidential and not to have discussions with any members of the defense team (including mental health professionals) unless explicitly authorized to do so by the retaining attorney.

POLICE-REQUESTED EVALUATIONS: CRIMINAL JUSTICE SYSTEM

Shortly after arrest or during the course of a police investigation, an individual charged with a particular offense may behave erratically or have memory difficulty, leading police or prosecutors to request a mental examination. At times, the individual may be brought to an emergency room for examination and treatment; a therapist may be asked to see the person at the police station or jail; or the individual may be brought to the therapist's office. If the nature of the therapist's role—whether conducting an examination or providing treatment for therapeutic purposes only—is not clarified at the outset, legal rights or professional ethical guidelines may be violated.

Police may try to use the emergency room evaluation, designed for treatment purposes, as a means of obtaining a confession.

For example, the police or the state's attorney often will press clinicians to reveal information, or will ask to observe the examination. Such requests should be refused. The American Psychiatric Association has declared that, except in emergencies, it is unethical to perform a police- or state-requested psychiatric examination before the defendant has obtained legal counsel (American Psychiatric Association, 1988). Emergency situations requiring examination and treatment—suicidal overdoses and acute psychotic states, among others—should be handled with the express understanding that the individual is a patient, with the same confidentiality guidelines that apply to any other patient. In these situations, the treating therapist should not act as an agent or consultant to the police, but should maintain the therapist-patient relationship to avoid the double agentry difficulties mentioned earlier.

CIVIL EVALUATIONS

Although the criminal justice system is often considered the epitome of the adversarial system, courts with jurisdiction over noncriminal, or civil, disputes are also adversarial in design. While civil cases permit more discovery of facts and opinions prior to the trial (through depositions and disclosure of reports), their process is no less adversarial and no less a threat to the therapist-patient dyad. In some areas of civil law, such as child custody disputes, the "best interests of the child" doctrine is used by the court to override the usual confidential privilege between a therapist and a patient. Likewise, in cases involving psychic harm, a plaintiff who introduces his mental condition as an issue waives his right to keep prior mental health treatment confidential. (A therapist may become involved in civil cases because, without a diagnosis and treatment, there would be no case.) The mental health professional approached to consult with an attorney in a civil action should apply the same clinical principles and fundamental ethical questions regarding the role of the consulting therapist as those just described for the criminal justice system.

In many states, civil commitment hearings may appear less adversarial as the hospital often will not be represented by an attorney and the strict rules of evidence are not followed. In spite of these differences, the same clinical principles and fundamental ethical questions regarding the consultation need to be considered as are required for evaluations in criminal cases.

Attorneys representing patients in civil commitment hearings also may feel substantial role conflicts. Some attorneys feel that the patient's wishes must be advocated fully, in spite of the person's lack of competence or their "best interest." Such attorneys will cross-examine the expert or therapist vigorously and attempt to exclude data unfavorable to their position. Other attorneys will attempt to counsel the patient or mediate some of the patient's concerns with the staff. The American Bar Association's Model Code of Professional Responsibility does not demand a course of zealous advocacy. It notes that "the responsibilities of a lawyer may vary according to the . . . mental condition of a client . . . . Any mental or physical condition of a client that renders him incapable of making a considered judgment on his own behalf casts additional responsibilities upon his lawyer . . . . If a client under disability has no legal representative [a guardian], his lawyer may be compelled in court proceeding to make decisions on behalf of his client" (American Bar Association, 1983). This code allows attorneys to adopt differing roles and still be seen as acting ethically on behalf of their clients.

Judges may be more active in questioning therapists and patients when attorneys are not representing the hospital or family. The degree to which strict rules of evidence are followed in civil commitment hearings varies from state to state and so examining experts may not be allowed to testify about information derived from the patient's family. Here, family members are expected to testify directly and to be available for cross-examination.

In practice, the roles of therapist as treating professional and as consultant to the attorney frequently are combined during the course of a case. While the roles are complementary, there are times when they should be more clearly separated, or perhaps should be performed by separate professionals.

SUMMARY

The mental health professional has an established role in a variety of criminal and civil areas of jurisprudence and works on behalf of a variety of parties to a legal case. The clarity with which the role is both defined and approached, however, is critical to ensure both the dignity of the profession and the sanctity of the therapist-patient relationship. Mental health professionals, then, are cautioned to understand and distinguish between their clinical responsibilities toward patients and their civic responsibilities toward the legal system as expert consultants, avoiding the awkward and potentially damaging double agentry that can ensnare the incautious.

The next chapter will discuss some of the legal tests used by the law with examples of clinical problems.

REFERENCES

Ake v. Oklahoma, 470 U.S. 68 (1985)

American Bar Association. (1983). *Model rules of professional conduct—Canon 7*. Washington, DC: ABA.

American Psychiatric Association. (1988). *The principles of medical ethics with annotations especially applicable to psychiatry, 1988 edition*. Washington, DC: APA.

4

COMMON LEGAL TESTS

From time to time, a mental health professional will receive a call from an attorney, a mental health agency, or a court which requests the professional to render expert opinion in a legal proceeding. The mental health professional who accepts this medicolegal consulting role becomes an integral part of the legal process. Among the first issues that arise when considering such a consultancy is the nature of the legal problem. Expert testimony from a trained practitioner generally centers around a specific legal test in which the mental capacity of the defendant, in a criminal action, or the plaintiff, in a civil action, is in question.

This chapter briefly addresses a number of the more common legal tests that require mental health expertise and provides two case examples using the questions of both insanity and competency. More detailed information relating to each specific area may be found in reference manuals (e.g., Albert, 1986; Goldzband, 1982, 1988; Gutheil & Appelbaum, 1982; Halleck, 1980; Sadoff, 1988; Schetky & Benedek, 1980; Simon, 1987). Readers are also referred to Appendix C.

TOPICS ON WHICH MENTAL HEALTH EXPERTISE MAY BE SOUGHT

Criminal Responsibility/Insanity Defense

Expert witnesses may be called upon to evaluate the capacity of an individual to control conduct and to understand the wrongfulness of acts at the time of an alleged offense. The inability either to control conduct or to appreciate wrongfulness of illegal acts stand as reasons that mitigate against legal guilt. Traditional legal tests such as the M'Naghten Rule, "irresistible impulse," and the model penal code form the basis for these evaluations.

Diminished Capacity/Extreme Emotional Disturbance

In criminal law, "intent" is an important factor, which may determine the type or degree of offense for which the defendant will be charged. Mental illness can impair intent to such a degree as to limit a homicide from murder in the first degree to second degree murder or manslaughter. The expert may be asked whether the defendant's capacity to have a specific intent (premeditation, malice, etc.) was impaired as the result of a mental disorder. A defendant unable to maintain the required intent, could then not be found guilty of that level of the crime. (First degree murder may be reduced to manslaughter, for example.) This is a very difficult concept and requires careful guidance by both the attorney and the forensically trained colleague. Mental illness alone does not necessarily rob a defendant of a specific intent. Extreme emotional disturbance is a different, but similar defense used in several states and applies only to first degree murder. If proven that a murder was committed under "extreme emotional disturbance," the charge is reduced to second degree murder. Generally, however, the defendant's emotional condition, short of legal insanity, is more relevant at the sentencing phase. Extreme mental impairment as the result of substance abuse may also legally affect criminal intent in rare cases.

Competency

Whether an individual can function and participate in a meaningful way is at the heart of competency issues spanning both the criminal and civil areas of the law. However, the issue of competency is relative to the task to be performed; it is not an absolute. Thus, by virtue of a mental disorder, a person may not be competent to manage finances, but may be competent to execute a will. Three common elements underlie nearly all competency issues: understanding of available choices, capacity to make those choices, and freedom from undue influence. In the criminal justice system, the question of competency arises in such areas as standing trial, being a witness, being executed, being paroled or placed on probation, and making a confession. Mental health experts may be called to evaluate competency in such civil areas as capacity to make a contract, adoption, and will writing.

Sentencing

Mental health professionals can aid a court's effort to determine a disposition by conducting general assessments, focusing, for example, on the potential for rehabilitation or on mitigating factors dictating for or against a particular sentence. In capital punishment jurisdictions, questions may arise about future dangerousness and capacity for personality change, among others. Similarly, experts may be called in cases involving sexual psychopathology under state statutes specifically governing this criminal area.

Involuntary Hospitalization/Civil Commitment

Here, legal questions arise about the nature of the mental illness itself. Does the person in question pose a threat to him- or herself or others? What other treatment settings that may be less restrictive are available? Chapter 7 provides substantial detail on this medicolegal area.

Personal Injury

When an individual is injured, the degree of harm must be assessed if damages are to be awarded. Questions in such cases include: Are the mental problems claimed connected directly to the alleged trauma? Was the alleged trauma a contributing factor in a subsequent mental disorder? What is the nature of the mental conditions that have arisen as a result of the trauma? Questions of treatment and prognosis also become important. Specific rules must be applied in Workers' Compensation and Social Security disability evaluations.

An important issue in personal injury is whether or not the action of the person being sued was the "proximate cause" of the injury. Proximate cause is a conclusion of law that identifies a single cause of an injury to be the legally responsible cause. While the concept has its origin in the idea of the "nearest" (or most proximate) cause, that definition may be somewhat misleading. A cause is determined to be "proximate" if, under all the circumstances, we are willing to say that it is the cause most responsible for an injury, not that it is necessarily the most recent or the most direct cause. For example, an emergency room failure to diagnose child abuse might lead to a child being returned to a caretaker who later either seriously injures or kills the child. The direct cause of injury to (or death of) the child would be the actions of the caretaker; the faulty diagnosis, however, would be the "proximate" cause of the injuries (or death). Thus, the clinician would be responsible, notwithstanding the fact that he or she never touched the child in anger.

A personal injury case presents an example of some of the mental health issues. A mentally healthy, 26 year-old, single male was a passenger in a car whose driver swerved to avoid an oncoming car. The car ran off the road, sheared a telephone pole, and overturned. The patient saw everything happening and was helpless to prevent it. He was released from the hospital after treatment for minor cuts. Almost immediately after, he began to have recurrent nightmares, generalized anxiety, insomnia, anorexia, etc. Two weeks later, he observed a very serious accident in which at least one person was killed. He began to develop feelings of impending doom. At about the same time, he was having difficulties at home dealing with his parents' objections to his leaving home in order to live with his girlfriend. In a civil suit for damages, an important issue will be whether his symptoms were alone caused by the first accident, or partially by the second accident and/or his emerging independence.

Malpractice Cases

While mental health professionals are reluctant to testify against their peers, key issues in malpractice cases center on the question of prevailing standards of care and whether the practitioner met such standards. Case example: A 24-year-old, unmarried woman was admitted to a psychiatric service of a general hospital. She had developed severe psychotic symptoms and was started on a trial of antipsychotic medications. Several days after her admission, she was placed in a seclusion room in a highly agitated and psychotic condition, after having told the staff that she heard voices telling her to hurt herself. Four hours after being placed in seclusion, she was found in the room with her head wedged between the side rail and the mattress of her bed, unconscious, with no pulse, blood pressure, or respiratory function. During that period of nearly four hours, no staff member entered the patient's room or had any personal contact with her to assess her mental condition or to alleviate her agitation. At trial, expert testimony will be required to establish both the appropriate standard of care with regard to monitoring psychotic patients in seclusion, and the standard of care for creating a safe environment in seclusion rooms consistent with the frequency of patient monitoring.

Ethical Violations

Here the questions may involve malpractice as well, but the questions are put by licensing boards or professional societies that are inquiring into the conduct of a professional. The determinations of such a board or society will govern future capacity to practice the profession. Issues include standards of ethical conduct, degree of necessary supervision, or fraud.

Testamentary Capacity

The legal questions relate to the competency to execute a will, based on knowledge of one's property, of one's heirs, and of the fact that a will is being executed. Questions of undue influence during the time at which the will was executed also may arise. For example, Mr. Jones, an 84-year-old widower diagnosed with Alzheimer's disease, showed moderate dementia, forgetfulness, and intermittent paranoid fears. He could correctly identify the fact that he had three living children; he understood that his assets included a home and about $110,000 in the bank; and he understood the purpose of a will. Mr. Jones would be found to have testamentary capacity in spite of his deficits. However, if he chose to disinherit one son based on a paranoid delusion that the son was poisoning him, Mr. Jones could be found to lack testamentary capacity by the factfinder (judge or jury).

Guardianship/Conservatorship

Courts will want to know whether an individual is capable of self-care or of managing finances. For example, a 42-year-old man had been diagnosed as a chronic paranoid schizophrenic, had experienced 10 hospitalizations in the past 20 years, and had just been awarded a Social Security disability allotment. For several years, when not hospitalized, he had received funds regularly from a trust established by his mother. Although never declared incompetent, he usually mismanaged his funds, requiring frequent help from his friends because he could not budget his spending properly. He had to declare bankruptcy several years ago because he could not control his finances. Currently, his room and board are paid directly to the facility where he lives. Although he receives $100 per week to spend on incidentals, he often has to borrow for cigarettes by the end of the week. His therapist or a consulting therapist would tell Social Security that the patient is unable to handle his funds, enabling a third party to function as a payee who can mete funds out to the patient over the course of a month. Were the patient to inherit money from a relative, he would have to be declared incompetent to manage those funds and a guardian would be appointed.

Family Law Issues

Questions may arise at a number of family law levels, varying from child custody to child abuse, from sexual abuse to the termination of parental rights. Governing phrases in such legal questions include "the best interests of the child," "parental fitness," and "consequences for the child and parent," among others. For example, a 27-year-old man who abandoned his wife and 10-month-old baby six years ago, would now like to visit them. He has paid child support regularly and gave his wife a divorce shortly after he left to enable her to remarry. He made no previous attempts to visit the child until he heard that the child's stepfather was contemplating adoption. The court would like to know whether it would be in the best interests of this child to allow the biological father to visit after so long an absence. Concepts such as the importance of the psychological father versus the biological parent will need to be considered. It may be necessary to evaluate the father, stepfather, mother, and child. Some knowledge about previous court rulings in that jurisdiction in similar cases, obtained from the attorney, would also be helpful, as would such books as *Beyond the Best Interests of the Child* (Goldstein et al., 1973).

Treatment Rights

Legal issues may arise when a patient refuses treatment. Independent experts may be called upon to determine whether the patient in question is receiving adequate treatment, whether rejection of treatment is medically responsible, or whether the patient should be denied a right to refuse treatment. Frequently, such cases involve class actions for a group in a specific institutional setting, such as a state hospital.

CASE ILLUSTRATIONS

Insanity Defense

Questions involving the insanity defense revolve around the issue of how criminal responsibility is defined. The standards are defined in state statute and in case law. As in most legal tests, the definitions are often brief, yet their meaning has given rise to endless dispute.

The two most common standards that a mental health professional will encounter are the M'Naghten Rule, first clarified in England in 1843, and the American Law Institute's Model Penal Code standard (American Law Institute, 1962). The M'Naghten Rule originally read that:

> to establish a defense on the grounds of insanity, it must be clearly proved that, at the time of committing the act, the party accused was laboring under such a defect of reason, from disease of the mind, as not to know the nature and quality of the act he was doing; or, if he did know it, that he did not know he was doing what was wrong.

The American Law Institute test reads that:

> (1) A person is not responsible for criminal conduct if at the time of such conduct as a result of mental disease or defect, he lacks substantial capacity either to appreciate the criminality (wrongfulness) of his conduct or to conform his conduct to the requirements of the law, and (2) As used in this article, the terms "mental disease or defect" do not include an abnormality manifested only by repeated criminal or other antisocial conduct.

A recent survey of states indicates that 16 states use the M'Naghten Rule for legal insanity, and another four use it when coupled with the "irresistible impulse" test. (The latter involves the volitional and self-control aspects of behavior.) No state relies exclusively on the irresistible impulse test. Since the test used and the language surrounding its use may change from time to time, the wise mental health expert will consult with the referring attorney before undertaking an evaluation of insanity.

Until the Hinckley case, a majority of states and the federal courts used the Model Penal Code standard. Subsequent to that case, Congress passed legislation in 1984 that eliminated the volitional part of the Model Penal Code standard. The federal statute then adopted reads as follows:

> It is an affirmative defense to a prosecution under any federal statute that, at the time of the commission of the acts constituting the offense, the defendant as a result of a severe mental disease or deficit, was unable to appreciate the nature and quality or the wrongfulness of his acts. Mental disease or deficit does not otherwise constitute a defense. (USC, 1984)

Problems can arise when a mental health professional attempts to apply clinical knowledge of a defendant's mental state to one of the above legal formulae. The underlying issue is whether or not a person is to be held responsible for his or her behavior. Hence, while professionals in both law and medicine are involved, the question has substantial societal and political meaning. The expert witness is being asked to focus on several key areas within the brief sentence of the M'Naghten test that address the mental condition at the time of the alleged offense. Yet, what seems forthright can be quite complex.

> By way of illustration: Mr. X, a 42-year-old male, has walked around for four years with an idea that a certain person he encounters near his apartment means to do him harm. Mr. X began to observe and follow Mr. Y, who apparently walks by the apartment daily on his way to work. Mr. X believes that he receives threatening glances from Mr. Y at times. Mr. X began to collect information about Mr. Y, such as where he works, his habits, and his place of worship. At times, Mr. X strolls past the business where Mr. Y works to see if he is there. Over a period of a few months, according to Mr. X, "the pressure built up to an intolerable degree." Mr. X felt he could not continue under the status quo. He concealed a knife and entered the office of Mr. Y, claiming to be a job-seeker. When Mr. Y turned his back, Mr. X pulled his knife and stabbed Mr. Y in the chest. The victim survived and said that he had never seen Mr. X and had no idea who he was.

A clinician may conclude, without too much difficulty, that a diagnosis of some type of paranoid or schizophrenic disorder is present. However, a question may arise in the courtroom about the possibility of a paranoid personality. If this not uncommon diagnostic dispute arises, the prosecutor may argue that "no disease of the mind" was present under the M'Naghten test, on the grounds that a personality disorder is not a "disease of the mind." The prosecution's expert may have testified rightly that clinicians have yet to agree whether or not Axis II diagnoses are diseases of the mind.

More frequently, the act will be assessed under the premise that a disease of the mind had impaired the capacity to know that the act was wrong. The question usually is interpreted in a narrow sense. Hence, the question posed is whether Mr. X knew that stabbing Mr. Y was wrong. If Mr. X claimed that he had heard the voice of God telling him to stab Mr. Y, a command hallucination, the presumption for not knowing the act was wrong would be stronger. Without such hallucinations, the expert mental health witness might have to apply reasoning as to the specific relationship between Mr. X's mental illness and his attempt to kill Mr. Y.

Competency to Stand Trial

Competency to stand trial is an area of court work in which mental health expert assistance is sought on a relatively regular basis. The standard form of the test of whether a defendant is competent to stand trial is whether he or she is able to cooperate with counsel or appreciates the nature of the charges against him or her. Again, such simple directives may give rise to debate.

> Case: A man is accused of killing his roommate. No attempt was made to conceal the body. The man, believing himself to be an employee of the CIA, also believes he has "executed" a victim on order from that agency. In all other respects, his mental functioning and reasoning are clear; he achieves a superior score on intellectual assessment. He does not see his act as wrong, provides great detail about his thinking prior to the act, and insists on going to trial. Hence, his attorney is prevented from raising an insanity defense. Should this individual be viewed as competent to stand trial?

In this difficult case, the defendant could have raised the insanity defense. However, he either is not interested in such a defense or believes he has carried out an act for the agency for whom he works. No evidence supporting his belief to be a CIA agent has come forth. Seemingly, he knows the charges against him, can cooperate with his counsel, and yet he insists on entering a plea of not guilty. When told that he is likely to be found guilty on the evidence available if he enters a plea of not guilty, he accepts the comment, but tolerantly adds that this may be the plan of the "agency."

To argue the absence of competency, an expert witness would need to address the nature of the man's mental illness—whether this is a limited, but systematic, type of delusional thinking. The expert would have to demonstrate further how the illness affects the defendant's capacity to participate in a trial.

SUMMARY

The nature of the legal test for which a mental health professional's advice is being sought will dictate the scope and breadth of the work to be done by that expert both before and during a court proceeding. While the vast majority of the tests are simple on their face, the expert must be wary of diverse legal interpretations of the tests. The answers demanded require not only sharp clinical insight, but also the capacity to capture the essence of the legal test at issue.

The next four chapters discuss the role of the treating mental health professional in relationship with the legal system.

REFERENCES

10 Cl. & F.200 Eng. Rep. 718 (H.L. 1843)

18 USC Sec. 20, 1984

Albert, R. (1986). *Law and social work practice.* New York: Springer.

American Law Institute. (1962). *Model penal code, Section 4.01* (Proposed official draft). Washington, DC: ALI.

Goldstein, J., Freud, A., & Solnit, A. (1973). *Beyond the best interests of the child.* New York: Macmillan.

Goldzband, M.G. (1982). *Consulting in child psychiatry*. Lexington, MA: Lexington Books.

Goldzband, M.G. (1988). *Custody cases and expert witnesses: A manual for attorneys* (2nd ed.). Clifton, NJ: Prentice Hall Law and Business.

Gutheil, T.G. & Applebaum, P.S. (1982). *Clinical handbook of psychiatry and the law*. New York: McGraw-Hill.

Halleck, S.L. (1980). *Law in the practice of psychiatry: A handbook for clinicians*. New York: Plenum.

Sadoff, R. (1988). *Forensic psychiatry* (2nd ed.). Springfield, IL: Charles C Thomas.

Schetky, D.H., & Benedek, E.P. (Eds.). (1985). *Emerging issues in child psychiatry and law*. New York: Brunner/Mazel.

Simon, R. (1987). *Clinical psychiatry and the law*. Washington, DC: American Psychiatric Press.

II

THE LAW, THE PATIENT, AND THE THERAPIST

5

THE THERAPIST IN COURT

Most therapists prefer the clinical setting to the courtroom. No professional enjoys appearing foolish in public or having his or her profession denigrated. The legal system's adversarial process often exposes an expert to attacks that challenge credibility as a professional. From a scientific standpoint, the legal rules of evidence often appear to withhold significant clinical data and opinion from the jury. Moreover, court appearances disrupt schedules and interfere with patients' needs. Nonetheless, patients and others do become enmeshed in problems that demand legal resolution utilizing expert mental health opinion. Indeed, the growing regulation of mental health practice by both legislation and case law makes it unlikely that today's clinician can avoid involvement in the judicial process altogether.

A courtroom bears little resemblance to a case conference in which a consensus is reached in free and open discussion with clinical colleagues. Rather, public confrontation, demands for specific data, and personal attacks upon competence and methodology place extraordinary demands and impose significant conflicts on the therapist. Mental health professionals usually are not aware of either the rules and procedures of the legal system or their possible role within it. Misunderstanding of the roles and obligations in the legal setting has led to embarrassment, ethical and legal violations of patient rights, harm to patients and practitioners, and negative public perception of the profession. Role confusion occurs when a past or current therapeutic relationship exists between an expert witness and an individual who becomes the subject of a forensic inquiry.

This chapter briefly explores those aspects of involvement in the legal system that a treating clinician may find difficult to square with the therapeutic role.

THERAPIST-EXPERT WITNESS ROLE CONFLICTS

The potential for role confusion is enhanced when a therapist is confronted by a forensic question about an individual with whom there has been a therapeutic relationship. Unless the request is simple and congruent with the therapeutic goals of treatment, it is generally advantageous to have the forensic evaluation performed by another expert who is not involved therapeutically. Although the rationale for this may not be immediately apparent, the nature of the forensic evaluation will often conflict with therapeutic goals and confidentiality. Possible conflicts include the following issues:

Before any mental health professionals may provide expert court testimony on behalf of a patient, they must be able to state that their opinions reflect a standard of "reasonable medical certainty/probability." This is a legally established standard with variable judicial interpretations. Any testimony discussing "possibilities" will be excluded from court proceedings. The "reasonable medical certainty" threshold must be reached before experts are permitted to articulate the basis of their opinion. The standard is not synonymous with the standard of proof "beyond a reasonable doubt." Few medical opinions reach the level of beyond a reasonable doubt. This reasonable medical (psychological) certainty requirement limits the conclusions reached by an expert to those that could be shared by similar professionals, if presented with similar facts; that the conclusions are at least more likely than not to be correct. Consensus suggests that reasonable medical certainty/probability is the same level of certainty that characterizes determinations to engage in a particular form of treatment for a given patient. Reasonable medical certainty is a legal standard, not a clinical standard. Testimony is not supposed to be speculative or mere possibility or represent the expert's idiosyncratic ideas (Rappeport, 1985). In clinical work, the therapeutic resolution of an unclear diagnostic problem usually does not require so formal and specific a pronouncement.

Most forensic evaluations require the gathering of data from a number of other sources, such as, family, employers, schools, and police, so that credibility and conclusions made by an expert witness are strengthened. Data from the individual alone, while important, usually is insufficient for forensic purposes. Such contacts and interviews with family members and employers may disrupt individual psychotherapy.

If the therapist takes on the role of the forensic expert, it may hinder consideration of the psychological impact of the legal process upon the individual. The legal issues may dominate the therapy to the exclusion of other important therapeutic work.

If the evaluation is not congruent with the patient's views, the therapeutic alliance may be compromised.

The therapist is usually privy to a great deal of detailed, personal, unrelated material that may be difficult to exclude if the therapist appears as a witness.

Especially complicated situations arise when the clinician is employed as a consultant in a jail or prison. As the primary obligation is to provide treatment, the clinician generally owes this group of patients the same confidentiality that would be provided to any patient. Reporting escape plans illustrates some of the divided loyalty issues in these settings, but such exceptions should be made clear during the first contacts. A therapist employed by a jail with treatment responsibilities would be acting inappropriately if involved in an evaluative role for the prosecutor without the patient's informed consent.

Another source of frequent confusion arises when a therapist, who is contacted or subpoenaed by an attorney, is unclear whether the forensic role to be played is as a *factual* or *expert* witness. The two are significantly different; the latter may jeopardize the therapeutic relationship seriously. As a factual witness, the therapist may be asked to describe the course of the patient's treatment, the diagnosis, or other clinical observations based on the medical record. The factual witness should not venture an expert opinion on the legal question to be resolved. In contrast, the expert witness (discussed in greater detail in Part III) generally maintains no clinical (treatment) relationship to the person for whom expert testimony is being solicited, undertakes an independent examination of the "client," and bills the attorney or other requesting party for time as an expert.

Nevertheless, many attorneys and judges believe that the therapist is a better witness than a consulting expert and is less likely to be impeached as a "hired gun," since the patient consulted the clinician for treatment rather than for presentation of expert opinion in court. While, in some areas of the country with limited numbers of mental health practitioners, the therapist may have the role of forensic expert thrust upon him, ordinarily, it is wise to avoid mixing the therapeutic and forensic expert roles. To the greatest extent possible, the expert should tease apart therapeutic and forensic work in an effort to segregate the roles and obligations of each and to maintain the appropriate role with the patient.

GENERAL ROLE ISSUES

Being in a nontherapeutic role poses questions for the individual clinician as well as for the profession. With the return of capital punishment, for example, the role of mental health professionals in capital sentencing hearings or in competency to be executed proceedings must be defined legally, professionally, and ethically. Individual values regarding the death penalty may preclude involvement in certain trials, hearings, or testimony for the prosecution where the death penalty is a possible punishment. In general, any personal bias that might affect the nature of the report should be made clear prior to the consultation.

A frequently discussed role conflict arises under the rubric of the expert as "detective." The credibility of the expert witness will be based upon the thoroughness of the evaluation as well as on the witness's experience and educational credentials. Generally, the person being evaluated is seen as having a strong interest in the outcome and, therefore, is less credible if his or her version alone has been accepted by the expert. For that reason, usually it is important to confirm the defendant's story through police reports and confessions, or with the family, employers, or other significant persons. Similarly, psychological testing is often useful to assist in reaching a diagnosis. The line between gathering appropriate confirmatory data and becoming a policeman is not easily drawn.

SUMMARY

When performing a forensic evaluation or providing direct consultation to the court or attorney, the expert is not in a therapeutic role. In fact, the outcome to a specific plaintiff or defendant may be harmful in some social or psychological sense. The defendant may be imprisoned, lose custody of a child, be found negligent, or suffer financial losses. A patient's therapist, therefore, should be extremely careful before agreeing to act as an "expert" witness for that patient. Except in limited circumstances, where the issues are minor and do not conflict with therapeutic goals, it is preferable to refer the patient to another professional for such evaluations. While the court has the final determination regarding acceptance of a clinician as an expert in any proceeding, the individual clinician, too, bears some responsibility not to add to role confusion. Notwithstanding the difficulties and confusions, the mental health professional can perform an important function in a variety of legal proceedings that, with care, will not interfere with the course of treatment.

Succeeding chapters in this section describe the treating clinician's role in meeting specific legal needs and requests of a patient.

REFERENCE

Rappeport, J. (1985). Reasonable medical certainty. *Bulletin of the American Academy of Psychiatry and Law, 13*, 5–15.

6

LEGAL ISSUES ARISING IN A TREATMENT RELATIONSHIP

Forensic issues requiring the awareness of the therapist arise repeatedly in the treatment situation. In general, the range of legal issues involving patients spans three major areas: legal issues inherent in the treatment process, legal entitlements, and legal issues arising incident to treatment. Treatment or patient management issues arise in such legal areas as informed consent, guardianship, testamentary capacity, commitment, suicide, and "duty to warn" (Mills et al., 1987). The therapist may be called upon to furnish reports that constitute a major component in determining a patient's legal entitlement to such benefits as Workers' Compensation, Social Security Disability Insurance, or damage awards for a personal injury. A report from the therapist also may be required to assist a patient who, during the course of treatment, suffers an unrelated loss, such as in child custody or in civil wrongs for which the patient is held responsible. This chapter touches briefly on each of these areas of clinical legal interface to assist the clinician in both identifying and addressing them.

LEGAL ISSUES RELATED TO TREATMENT

Informed Consent

Today, the issue of informed consent has become paramount. Before a competent patient can be treated, the patient must give consent. This means that the patient must understand the risks and benefits of the treatment, its purpose and goals, the duties of the patient and therapist, and the available alternative treatments. This is the informed part of informed consent. Obviously, only a competent person can give a valid consent.

Should the patient be considered incompetent, that is, unable to understand the information, a substitute consent-giver is required. Depending on the jurisdiction and the patient's condition, this substitution will vary. It may require only the patient's statement to let a spouse decide, or it may require a formal court hearing first to determine incompetency and then to appoint a guardian.

The necessity of informed consent for antipsychotic medication is of particular importance when side-effects of long-term use are possible. The patient should be told about the potential risk of tardive dyskinesia. Some believe this should be done before medication is begun when such knowledge is an important factor in determining whether to take or to refuse the medication. Others discuss these problems once the patient is stabilized and is able to understand a discussion about this condition. Some authorities believe that a signed consent form is preferable to a written note in the record that the patient has been informed and has understood. Other authorities say that such forms are of little legal value; the use of a consent form, then, is an individual or institutional decision. Repeated and documented disclosure may be necessary to assure patient understanding. What is important is that the patient understand the risks and benefits of and alternatives to all treatments offered, and that a record is made indicating that the patient understood the information and agreed or refused the treatment.

Guardianship

Therapists will encounter the issue of guardianship when treating patients with progressive dementia or other severely disabling conditions such as AIDS, Alzheimer's disease, schizophrenia, or manic depressive disorders (including bipolar patients with manic excessive spending). Each jurisdiction has its own legal requirements governing the establishment of power of attorney or guardianship when a patient is unable to manage finances or self-care (Gutheil & Applebaum, 1982). It is important to plan ahead with the patient to discuss the possibility of assistance through power of attorney or guardianship while the patient remains able to understand these matters.

Should a therapist attempt to have a guardian appointed over a patient's objection? This dilemma might arise when the therapist believes a patient may not be competent to manage his or her own affairs. Failure to do so may result in harm to the patient; an affirmative decision may damage irrevocably the clinician-patient relationship. A decision in this difficult situation may be facilitated by consultation with more experienced colleagues. Further, an attorney should be consulted about the jurisdiction's rules governing guardianship, the observations that need to be made, and the forms that need to be completed.

Suicide

Suicidal patients pose a particular management problem for the therapist. While for the most part there are no laws against committing suicide, the therapist has a duty to the patient to prevent suicide whenever possible. When the therapist believes that a patient is suicidal and the patient refuses hospitalization, commitment becomes one option. When commitment is not instituted, a consultation should be obtained. Two heads, in this case, are better than one, when deciding whether there is a reasonable risk in continuing outpatient treatment.

Some therapists attempt to manage the patient by establishing an oral or written contract against suicide. Still others ask the patient to agree to call the therapist if the desire to commit suicide becomes overwhelming. Unfortunately, all patients do not abide by such contracts. Thus, contracts, in contrast to commitment, may be of limited value in either preventing suicide or in defending against a later malpractice claim. The therapist should record the evaluation of a patient's suicidal intent in the record, explaining the decision either to maintain outpatient treatment or to attempt commitment.

Tarasoff Warnings

Since the late 1970s, following the Tarasoff case in California (Mills et al., 1987), the law in many jurisdictions affirms that clinicians owe a duty to known third parties to prevent harm by a patient. While historically we are not our brother's keepers, the courts have ruled that the special relationship between therapist and patient may generate a duty to an endangered third party. This duty, originally called the "duty to warn," has been supplanted by a broader concept—the "duty to protect" (*Tarasoff v. Regents*, 1976). Thus, the therapist has a duty to try to prevent a patient from harming a known individual. In several cases in which a specific, known individual was not at risk, courts have found that the capacity to foresee danger to the public at large was so great that a therapist owed a duty to protect even unknown persons (*Lipari v. Sears*, 1980). Ordinarily, the protection can be accomplished by hospitalizing the dangerous patient, by taking other management steps, or even by arranging a therapeutic confrontation between the patient and the potential victim. Some states now specify the limits of a therapist's duty to protect third parties and how these duties may be satisfied. A prudent clinical response to the dangerous patient is always essential (Beck, 1985). An APA Task Force has issued a report on the Tarasoff issue as it affects the clinician (Applebaum et al., 1989).

Right to Refuse Treatment

Each jurisdiction maintains its own rules for determining a patient's right to refuse treatment, a concept that, in practice, has come to mean the right to refuse medication. In outpatient practice, the right to refuse treatment is seldom an issue. A patient can stop treatment, can be noncompliant, or simply can refuse to take medication, although harm from the refusal may happen to the patient or another person. In an inpatient setting, however, the problem becomes more complex, since harm resulting from treatment refusal can come more readily to the patient, staff, or other patients. Several states require a series of judicial procedures to override refused treatment in nonemergency situations (Brakel et al., 1985). The other states permit internal review procedures, based on second opinions or decisions by hospital-based committees, to determine whether the patient should be allowed to refuse proposed treatment. In any case, a note should be placed in the patient's record indicating that treatment was refused.

LEGAL ISSUES REGARDING ENTITLEMENT TO BENEFITS

The law has established several different entitlement systems that may benefit patients. These include Workers' Compensation for those injured on the job, Social Security Disability Insurance for those unable to work due to mental disability, and damage awards for personal injury. In the last case, civil law allows individuals to receive compensatory damages and, sometimes, punitive damages when injured through no fault of their own. On occasion, a therapist may be asked to prepare an evaluation of a current patient for one of these entitlement programs.

Workers' Compensation

The Workers' Compensation system, developed in the early 1900s, allows workers to receive compensation from work-related disabilities in an uncomplicated, equitable fashion. Simply stated, it is a special insurance system for which we all pay. A few cents are added to everything we purchase, establishing a pool of money to be paid out to workers injured on the job. The amount of money received by the worker, the attorney, or the treating professional is controlled; no payment is made for pain and suffering or loss of consortium. To compensate the worker, a fee schedule has been established, based on the extent of disability (loss of functional ability), the future earning capacity, and the permanence of the injury.

When a patient is injured on the job or is in treatment because of the emotional sequelae of an injury, the therapist can be certain the patient's attorney will want a report. This report should describe the impairment, discuss whether it is temporary or permanent, and delineate whether the resultant disability is partial or total. (See Appendix F.) The Workers' Compensation Commission may require the findings to be expressed in percentages or in the degree of impairment of the whole person (for example, diagnosis: Post-Traumatic Stress Disorder, Partial, Temporary, 30% impaired in skills of daily living). It is important to remember that the patient will see the report, and that seeing it could interfere with treatment. Guidance from a colleague or the patient's attorney is advised for the therapist who is inexperienced in Workers' Compensation reporting requirements. Brodsky (1987) has provided an outline detailing what should be included in a therapist's Workers' Compensation evaluation, and, the Council on Occupational Health of the American Medical Association has developed a useful step-by-step volume to assist the therapist in determining the degree of disability (Engelberg, 1988). A consultant other than the therapist may be called upon by the company to evaluate the claimant's injury.

Social Security Disability Insurance

The chronically mentally ill patient may be eligible for Social Security Disability Insurance (SSDI), and, if so, two years later for Medicaid benefits. Such patients also may be eligible for Supplemental Security Income (SSI), whether or not they were ever employed and are now benefiting from other social programs. Application for these benefits should not be taken lightly, since the standards required are the most stringent of any entitlement program in the nation's history (Dilley, 1987). The state Disability Determination Service (DDS), under contract with the Social Security Administration, is responsible for initial SSDI determinations. When a claim is filed, the DDS will request a report from the clinician. The agency generally requires a complete history and details that describe fully the patient's functional capacity (whether the patient may be gainfully employed in any capacity). The agency also needs to know the disability and an estimate of how long the condition causing the disability will continue.

It is essential that the clinical report should be sufficiently detailed to enable another professional, who is not necessarily expert in mental illness and has no knowledge of the patient, to review the report and make a determination of benefit entitlement. Otherwise, a deserving patient could be refused disability benefits, necessitating a long and arduous reconsideration and further appeals in order to receive benefits. The Social Security Administration has published several articles and pamphlets that spell out the types of clinical information most helpful in the SSDI determination process. Krajeski and Lipsett (1987) provide a road map to the SSDI mental impairment evaluation for the clinician who is called upon by a state DDS to provide a report on a patient. Consultation with a colleague experienced in the SSDI examination process may also be of help in such cases.

LEGAL ISSUES THAT ARISE DURING TREATMENT

Acts Against Society

People suffering from psychiatric disorders may engage in acts against society that result in criminal charges. These acts can occur when a person is already in treatment. Alternatively, an individual may seek treatment because of trouble with the law. A request for treatment by an individual in legal difficulty may be a genuine sign of emotional distress or may be a manipulative act. The therapist should try to understand why a prospective patient is seeking help.

Some therapists believe that there are advantages to therapy conducted while a patient has charges pending; others do not believe involvement with a patient is warranted under these circumstances. Still other therapists are willing to treat a patient while charges are pending as long as the patient does not request a written report from the therapist. Difficulties may arise with this last approach. A patient may agree to the therapist's conditions at the outset, but later may insist on a report. At that time, the therapist may find it difficult to refuse to furnish a report. If the therapist refuses to furnish a report, the therapist can be subpoenaed and possibly required to testify. Further, problems may arise when the therapist becomes the patient's advocate, particularly if the therapist is privy to information that may complicate the patient's interaction with the criminal justice system. Under these circumstances, it is desirable to consult a colleague experienced in dealing with the conflicting roles of the treating professional in the forensic arena.

Wills

Testamentary capacity is a person's ability to write a will. This forensic issue may arise in treatment when a patient tells the therapist that the preparation of a will is being contemplated or has just been completed. Under such circumstances, the therapist should note a series of observations in the record regarding the patient's testamentary capacity. To be competent to execute a will, an individual must know three things: 1) the nature of the document being signed; 2) the limits and extent of what is owned; and 3) the natural objects of his or her bounty (who by law and natural relationship should receive some of the property, such as spouse or children). In discussing these matters with the patient, the clinician should note in the record whether the patient meets the tests for testamentary capacity.

Should a therapist be concerned about this matter? The answer is yes. Imagine that a wealthy patient in treatment for a paranoid disorder tells you that he has decided to exclude his children from his new will, based on his delusional ideas. Were this patient to die, excluded children could sue the estate, alleging a right to a portion of the patient's estate. In such a situation, the therapist might want to consult his own lawyer or a forensic mental health professional. In any situation in which the deceased had been under mental health care, the likelihood of such a suit is increased. Under these circumstances, a note in the record regarding the patient's testamentary capacity when the will was written helps preserve the patient's wishes after death.

An attorney who is writing a will for a client and knows that his or her client is receiving mental health care should request the patient's permission to speak with the therapist about the issue of testamentary capacity. The therapist should discuss with the attorney how a report by the therapist may impact on the therapy. If it will interfere, then a forensic consultation for testamentary capacity should be obtained.

Personal Injury

From time to time, an individual suffers an injury caused by someone else, such as injury in an automobile accident. In some circumstances, the accident may precipitate the psychiatric consultation; in other circumstances, the accident may occur while the patient is already in treatment. The therapist owes the patient a duty to furnish reports when requested by the patient's attorney. The reports allow others to make required determinations of damages that may have been sustained.

Development of such reports may compromise the therapeutic relationship. Nevertheless, the patient maintains the right to request and to obtain such a report. Thus, when formulating the report, the therapist should strive for objectivity. It is neither fair to the patient to belittle or minimize the injuries, nor is it fair to the patient or others to exaggerate the injuries. A patient may desire, or an overly helpful therapist may be tempted, not to be objective. Even though such lack of objectivity may not destroy the therapeutic relationship, can a patient ever again really trust a therapist who has lied?

Commitment

Sometimes it is necessary to commit a patient to the hospital. Commitment laws usually authorize involuntary treatment only if the patient refuses voluntary hospitalization, meets certain statutory criteria, and a less restrictive alternative is not available. Specific forms must be completed, and hearings must be attended. At such hearings, the need for commitment is tested in an adversarial forum. Every expert witness should be familiar with the appropriate state's commitment laws. Commitment should never be undertaken lightly, but when commitment is necessary, it must be undertaken properly. Chapter 7 provides detailed information about both the form and the process of civil commitment.

Divorce and Custody

Individuals in treatment occasionally are involved in divorce and custody disputes. The therapist is called upon to render an opinion about the patient's parenting abilities. Moreover, the therapist may be called upon by an adverse attorney on a "fishing expedition," looking for information to help a patient's spouse obtain custody. In either case, the release of information can destroy the therapeutic relationship.

On occasion, the therapist is served a subpoena for records believed to be relevant in a former patient's custody dispute. It is important for the former patient and the patient's attorney to review the salient treatment files in order to be sure they know the contents. If couples therapy occurred or if the patient's spouse was evaluated as an informant, the therapist's records may contain material either damaging or helpful to both parties. At times, therapists may need to call on a forensically trained colleague or on their own legal counsel when deciding whether to testify or to release records in divorce and custody proceedings involving a current or former patient. The same recourse may be necessary when a request for family therapy records is made. Suggesting an independent evaluation may be a useful alternative.

CONFIDENTIALITY AND PRIVILEGED COMMUNICATIONS

Throughout the foregoing discussion, the issues of confidentiality and privilege arise as a threat to the clinician and patient alike. Confidentiality is an ethical responsibility of the therapist not to reveal to others what is communicated in the therapeutic relationship. Privilege is the patient's right to prevent testimony by a therapist. What responsibility does a therapist have to maintain confidentiality under these varied circumstances? Almost all jurisdictions limit the privilege a patient may claim once the patient's mental state becomes a part of the legal proceedings in a criminal defense or in a civil suit brought by the patient. Under these circumstances, the therapist may be forced to furnish information that may not otherwise be revealed publicly. While such revelations may destroy the therapeutic relationship, it is the patient's decision whether or not to open the records to scrutiny. Once the records are open, the therapist is not always able to prevent harm to the patient. The same general problem arises when a therapist is asked to furnish information to insurance companies or to the disability determination offices.

Most recently, the proliferation of AIDS and concerns about child abuse have raised new issues of confidentiality. Mental health clinicians are now grappling with the limits of their responsibility to inform those who may have been exposed to AIDS or have told them of child abuse. Professional organizations and some states have promulgated guidelines and laws for clinicians dealing with these issues, which delineate the specific circumstances under which a breach of confidentiality is permitted.

SUMMARY

The foregoing represent but a few of the legal issues to which practicing clinicians are exposed as the result of both their relationships with their patients and the special nature of working with the mentally ill. The intensity with which the law oversees therapeutic relationships and makes inroads into them is in perpetual flux. The patients' rights movement appears to have peaked after a period of ascendancy. However, it is unlikely that society will ever return to the paternalistic position extant in the first half of this century. Today's therapist has a responsibility to inform the patient about treatment, including risks, benefits, limitations, and alternatives. The therapist has the further obligation to assist in the management of the patient's affairs (or in ensuring that someone else can manage them), to protect the patient from suicide, and to commit the patient to a hospital, when necessary. The therapist must meet legal requirements of right to refuse treatment statutes and at the same time must meet the duty to prevent a dangerous patient from harming others.

In most instances, the cautious therapist can assist the patient with the legal problems without sacrificing the therapeutic relationship. However, situations arise in which the patient must decide whether to chance destruction of the treatment relationship in order to "win" a legal dispute. As in all therapeutic situations, the therapist must strive to work in the best interests of the patient.

Issues related to civil commitment are discussed in the next chapter.

REFERENCES

Applebaum, P.S., Zonana, H., Bonnie, R. & Roth, L.H. (1989). Statutory approaches to limiting psychiatrists' liability for their patients' violent acts. *American Journal of Psychiatry, 146*, 821–828.

Beck, J.C. (Ed.). (1985). *The potentially violent patient and the Tarasoff decision in psychiatric practice.* Washington, DC: American Psychiatric Press.

Brakel, S.J., Parry, J. & Weiner, B. (1985). *The mentally disabled and the law* (3rd ed.). Chicago: American Bar Foundation.

Brodsky, C. (1987). The psychiatric evaluation in worker's compensation. In A.T. Meyerson & T. Fine (Eds.), *Psychiatric disability: Clinical, legal and administrative dimensions.* Washington, DC: American Psychiatric Press.

Dilley, P. (1987). Social security disability: Political philosophy and history. In A.T. Meyerson & T. Fine (Eds.), *Psychiatric disability: Clinical, legal and administrative dimensions.* Washington, DC: American Psychiatric Press.

Engelberg, A.L. (Ed.). (1988). *Guides to the evaluation of permanent impairment* (3rd ed). Chicago: American Medical Association.

Gutheil, T.G., & Applebaum, P.S. (1982). *Clinical handbook of psychiatry and the law.* New York: McGraw-Hill.

Krajeski, J., & Lipsett, M. (1987). The psychiatric consultation for social security disability. In A.T. Meyerson & T. Fine (Eds.), *Psychiatric disability: Clinical, legal and administrative issues.* Washington, DC: American Psychiatric Press.

Lipari v. Sears Roebuck & Co. 497 F.Supp 185 (D Neb 1980).

Mills, M.J., Sullivan, G., & Eth, S. (1987). Protecting third parties: A decade after Tarasoff. *American Journal of Psychiatry, 144*(1), 68–74.

Tarasoff v. Regents of the Univ. of California 551 P2d 334 (1976).

7

CIVIL COMMITMENT: THE THERAPIST'S ROLE

The legal process through which a patient is involuntarily hospitalized is perhaps the most common avenue through which the practicing clinician becomes involved in the judicial process. Because commitment results in the loss of a patient's personal liberty, the legal process that governs its implementation is both complex and exacting.

Historically, the balance between an individual's constitutional right to liberty and the state's obligation to protect the community and its mentally ill citizens has been in perpetual sway. British law held the King to have ultimate authority to act as "the general guardian of all infants, idiots, and lunatics" (*Hawaii v. Standard Oil*, 1972). By the mid-1800s, humanistic protection of mentally ill citizens and the community was affirmed through the introduction of involuntary hospitalization (*In the Matter of Josiah Oakes*, 1845). Traditionally, states relied on the legal tenet of *parens patriae*, the state's authority to act in the best interests of an individual found unable to care for him or herself. This doctrine has been a foundation for state laws that permit involuntary commitment of the mentally ill, establish guardianships, and protect the interests of minors. Constitutional requirements of substantive due process, demanding that all state actions be related to a valid state goal, place limits on the state's exercise of its parental power.

More recently, increased judicial priority on *police power* commitments in the 1960s has replaced the previous decade's legal emphasis on *parens patriae* commitment. Under police power commitment, the state exercises its inherent power to protect the health, safety, and welfare of its inhabitants. Included in this authority is the right to protect the community from the mentally ill and the mentally ill citizen from him or herself. A confinement based on this premise is not predicated on a prior criminal act and must not prove to be unduly oppressive. The state is required to prove the mentally ill citizen to be either a danger to self or others by at least the standard of clear and convincing evidence. Limiting commitments by the requirement of dangerousness has made it more difficult to hospitalize patients involuntarily.

The shift in emphasis from *parens patriae* to police power has generated a variety of differing state laws governing civil commitment criteria and procedures. Because we do not have a single, national civil commitment procedure, readers are urged to consult appropriate state civil commitment statutes. General legal principles regarding commitment and the unique role played by the mentally health professional in the commitment process are discussed below.

COMMITMENT CRITERIA

State laws governing involuntary psychiatric hospitalization generally require the individual in question to be gravely disabled and/or a danger to self or others as a result of a mental illness. Patients are usually also required to be placed in the least restrictive setting for treatment. In some jurisdictions, this includes commitment to outpatient treatment.

While all state commitment statutes require the presence of a mental illness, legal definitions of mental illness vary from the inability to exercise self-control to the general impairment of mental health. Psychiatric diagnosis and mental status examinations are helpful in providing the necessary objective evidence to meet this criterion.

Gravely Disabled

Gravely disabled is defined generally as the inability to provide for one's own basic needs. Legal criteria upon which grave disability are based include an insufficient capacity to make responsible decisions regarding hospitalization, an inability to care for or protect oneself, and a need for involuntary care.

Dangerousness

A judgment of dangerousness usually focuses on three factors: 1) the magnitude of harm likely to result from an act of violence; 2) the likelihood that a harmful act will be committed; and 3) the time span during which that act is likely to occur (Note: Harvard Law Review, 1974). An assessment of the magnitude of harm takes into account both predicted physical injury and potential property damage. Probability of harm is determined by evaluating the magnitude of the harm a person is predicted to cause and the likelihood that a person will engage in specific antisocial conduct that will result in harm.

The capacity of mental health professionals to accurately assess dangerousness is limited. The predictive accuracy of dangerousness determinations can be improved if greater attention is paid to the history of prior aggressive behavior and to careful evaluation of the presenting disorder.

Least Restrictive Setting

Involuntary commitment statutes in a number of states encourage placement in the least restrictive setting. This principle allows minimal infringement upon the individual right to liberty while facilitating appropriate treatment. Illinois and Ohio, for example, require that the "court must order the least restrictive alternative." Both New Mexico and Virginia specify identification of the least restrictive setting as a prerequisite to an involuntary treatment order. Private hospitals, nonresidential treatment programs, or outpatient commitment are among the available alternatives to inpatient psychiatric hospitalization.

COMMITMENT ROUTES

An individual is admitted to a psychiatric facility on an involuntary basis through one of three courses: emergency, judicial decision, or guardianship/conservatorship, though the last is available only in some jurisdictions. Of the three, the most common route is emergency detention. Playing a major role in such cases is the determination that, without immediate hospitalization, substantial harm would come to the patient or others. The authority to make such an assessment varies across the states, but it is generally restricted to mental health professionals and/or law enforcement personnel.

Emergency

Typically, at the time of emergency admission, when a written application in support of the involuntary hospitalization is submitted, the criteria upon which the commitment is based are stated clearly. Relevant facts about a patient's behavior, thought disorder, cognition, suicidality, homicidality, and self-care capacity are also outlined briefly. Unlike other commitment mechanisms, emergency commitment does not require judicial review prior to detention.

Judicial

Judicial commitment—commitment through the courts—is initiated in nonemergency situations, which allow a court to act prior to hospitalization. A written application, affidavit, or petition alleging the need for involuntary hospitalization is submitted to the court. In most states, anyone with knowledge of the facts may file such a petition. The document may include: descriptions of overt acts or threats (Illinois); personal information about the patient, including both family history and history of mental illness (Ohio, Illinois); and statements regarding the availability of treatment (Idaho). Depending on state statute, some of the foregoing statements are required to be made under oath.

States frequently require that medical certificates, completed by a recognized, qualified mental health professional, accompany the affidavit. State laws regarding the content of the certificate vary, but may require: a declaration that the originator has personally examined the patient; the examiner's clinical observations and conclusions (Illinois); the facts and circumstances supporting statements made in the certificate (New York); a statement of the relationship between the examiner and petitioner, affiant, or applicant (New Jersey); a declaration that the patient meets state commitment criteria (Oklahoma); or a statement that the patient has been advised of the right to remain silent (Illinois). Both the petition and the medical certificate may be subject to further screening by either the court or an independent mental health worker.

If the petition is found to be valid, the court may order a noncooperative mentally ill individual to be transported to the hospital. Once a court order is in hand, the individual may be taken into custody within 24 hours (North Carolina), on receipt of a warrant (Texas), or immediately (Ohio). In each case, a law enforcement officer detains the individual and initiates a "hold," later formalized by the hospital's examining mental health professional. Once detention is achieved, a full hearing is scheduled before a judge or judicially appointed referee.

Guardian or Conservator

In some states, a guardian or conservator may initiate psychiatric hospitalization without prior judicial approval. Usually, a family member is granted guardianship or conservatorship when a relative is found to be legally incompetent. The guardian or conservator is empowered to arrange for housing, personal care, and treatment of the designated individual. Both the process through which one is designated a conservator or guardian and how the status is maintained over time vary from state to state.

NOTICE

All commitment proceedings require the patient to be notified of many relevant statutory and due process rights. However, issues of how, when, by whom, and to whom the notice should be given vary widely across the country. For example, timing of the notice may be based on the time of custody, the initiation of psychiatric evaluation or treatment, the date of admission to a facility, the appointment of an attorney, or even the hearing date. Similarly, notice may be presented to the legal counsel, a mental health advocacy group, a relative or guardian, or the patient himself. The official responsible for serving notice may be a court officer, the director of a hospital, the head of community services, a police officer, or a designated mental health professional. Notification of rights (other than those regarding due process) may include information about telephone access probable cause hearing, or rights regarding medications. The following is a more detailed, albeit incomplete, list showing the range of rights accorded patients in different states in 1984 taken from Van Duizend et al. (1984).

SOME PATIENT RIGHTS ISSUES

General

Right to keep personal possessions (California)

Access to telephone or opportunity to leave written note (Ohio, California)

Access to an interpreter (California)

Same protections and rights of persons already committed (Idaho)

Reasonable number of telephone calls to reach attorney, physician, or licensed clinical psychologist (Ohio)

Statement of reason or purpose for detention (California, New Mexico)

Legal

Clear and concise statement of legal status (Illinois)

Hearing within a specified number of days (Iowa, New Mexico, New York, Massachusetts)

Hearing before a judge (California)

Right to a jury trial (Oklahoma)

Probable cause or preliminary hearing (Ohio, Connecticut, Massachusetts)

Right to be present at hearing (Massachusetts, Iowa)

Right to assistance of counsel (California, Ohio, Massachusetts)

Maximum length of detention (California)
Copy of application or petition (Massachusetts)
Examination by a mental health professional (Massachusetts, Iowa, California)
Right to remain silent during examination (Illinois)
Duty to remain in jurisdiction (Iowa)
Time and place of mental health examination (Iowa)

Treatment

Right to necessary and appropriate treatment (New Mexico, California)
Right to refuse medication (Illinois)
Availability of medical and psychiatric assistance (Ohio)
Independent mental health examination (Massachusetts, New Mexico, Iowa, Ohio)

PREHEARING EXAMINATION

Prehearing examinations are usually performed by a psychiatrist, psychologist, or other authorized professional at the time of admission. The examination may range in detail from a multidisciplinary professional analysis to a simply completed checklist. States may require mental status examinations to be preceded by a notification of rights and an explanation of the nature, purpose, and consequences of the examination.

PROBABLE CAUSE HEARING

The preliminary decision to hospitalize a patient involuntarily may be reviewed in a probable cause hearing. Typically, a probable cause hearing is held at the mental health facility and led by a court-appointed referee. While not a full review of the patient's condition and need for treatment, it is designed to make sure that there is competent evidence to warrant hospitalization. The meeting is generally informal and is attended by the patient, relatives, patient advocate, court representative, and designated mental health professional. Often, medical and nursing students and members of the general public are permitted entry only when patient consent has been received. During the hearing, the patient advocate or representative of the public guardian's office may ensure that correct commitment procedure has been followed. At the patient's request, the advocate may speak on behalf of the patient.

COMMITMENT HEARING

A commitment hearing, officiated by a judge or hearing officer, takes place at a courthouse or hospital. While less formal than a criminal trial, the patient becomes a respondent and is represented by an attorney. A State facility may be represented by the attorney general's office, though in practice, the treatment team often stands alone to present evidence that supports the commitment. Although cross-examination is limited, the expert witness should anticipate questions about both professional credentials and prior court experience. The expert should present the relevant facts in the context of the commitment criteria and without exaggeration of symptoms, embellishment of case history, or inclusion of lengthy differential diagnoses. The reader is referred to Chapter 13 for further information about behavior at court proceedings.

Other common legal rights are applicable to the civil commitment process. The patient has the right to attend his own hearing, though he may be excused if the court determines that attendance would be detrimental to his health. The individual also has the right to appointed or selected counsel unless voluntarily and knowingly waived. In practice, however, courts are reluctant to recognize a waiver of the right to counsel as valid when impaired judgment is suspected. Many state laws include the right to a jury trial, though courts have not yet determined whether jury trial is a requirement for due process in civil commitment cases. If the court finds by clear and convincing evidence that the respondent meets the criteria for commitment, the hospitalization will be continued; otherwise the patient will be released.

THERAPEUTIC IMPLICATIONS

Within the adversarial atmosphere of the legal proceeding, the clinician should maintain a therapeutic demeanor. Often, involuntary status is central to the patient's concerns. Hence, an open discussion with the patient, exploring the patient's perceptions of hospitalization and any ambivalence about inpatient care, is essential to diffuse the anger and correct the misconceptions that may erode the therapeutic alliance. Further, the patient should be reassured that both treatment plan and staff attitudes will not be altered by a decision to contest the proceeding. If the patient requires medication, it should be titrated to ensure that the patient is neither oversedated during the proceedings nor undermedicated to exacerbate symptoms on the day of the hearing.

SUMMARY

Involuntary psychiatric hospitalization represents a deprivation of one's constitutional right to liberty and freedom. *Parens patriae* and police power commitments attempt a compromise between the right to individual liberty and the general welfare of the society as a whole. Criteria for commitment include conditions that are often difficult to define or to predict: the presence of a mental illness, grave disability, or dangerousness to self or others. To justify involuntary hospitalization, courts must find commitment criteria to meet at least the standard of "clear and convincing evidence." An understanding of the legal issues inherent in civil commitment is essential to the mental health professional who chooses to meet the challenge of providing involuntary psychiatric care.

REFERENCES

Note: Developments in the law—Civil commitment of the mentally ill. *Harvard Law Review*. 87:1190, p. 1300, 1974.

Hawaii v. Standard Oil Co., 405 U.S. 251, 257 (1972), quoting B. W. Blackstone, Commentaries 47.

In the Matter of Josiah Oakes, 8 Law Reporter 122 124–25 (Mass. 1845).

Van Duizend, R., McGraw, B., & Keilitz, I. (1984). An overview of state involuntary civil commitment statutes. *Mental and Physical Disability Law Reporter*, *8*, 330.

8

LEGAL REQUESTS AND THE SUBPOENA

By tradition, the therapist/patient relationship is considered protected. Therapists embrace the long-standing values contained in the Hippocratic oath and incur obligations to maintain confidentiality for their patients. Communications are made in private and are expected to be held in confidence. Usually, patient and therapist voluntarily choose engagement in the treatment partnership; each affirmatively selects the other. When the needs of society and the legal system intrude, the nature of the therapeutic relationship may change since forensic evaluations can conflict with both therapeutic goals and confidentiality. Unless the legal request is simple and does not compromise treatment objectives (as in some welfare or Social Security disability requests), it is generally advantageous for a forensic evaluation to be performed by a mental health professional other than the treating professional. Nonetheless, occasions arise in which a patient's therapist is presented with solicitations for patient-related information from a court, an attorney or an official body.

CALLS

The patient's attorney may place an informal telephone call to request the therapist's cooperation in a legal matter. The friendly informality of the communication should not lead the therapist to forget the formal nature of the treatment relationship and the potential effect of the legal communication on that relationship. Discussion with the attorney should occur only after the therapist is satisfied that the attorney is acting with the patient's permission. However, when possible, it is desirable for the therapist to discuss the request with the patient beforehand. As detailed in the previous chapter, the therapist should discuss with the attorney and the patient any risk to treatment goals that may occur if records are to be disclosed.

When a telephone call is received from an attorney who represents a party other than the patient, the therapist should not discuss any matters involving a patient. Instead, the matter should be referred immediately to the patient's attorney.

LETTERS

A therapist may receive letters with accompanying signed blanket releases that authorize disclosure of treatment records. The letter's author may be the patient, the patient's attorney, or opposing legal counsel. If such a communication arrives unexpectedly, the therapist and patient or therapist and patient's attorney should discuss the matter. The therapist must be certain that release of information has been authorized legally by the patient and also must be clear about the scope of data to be released. The patient and the patient's attorney deserve to know what information will be provided. If records are sought, the therapist should offer to provide a summary instead. However, frequently the patient's attorney will need to review all records and notes in order to prepare for trial. In that event, the material should be copied and sent.

Letters received from attorneys with interests adverse to those of a patient should be managed with great care. The patient must know about the matter, and information should only be provided after consultation with the patient's counsel and then should be held to the minimum necessary to satisfy the request.

PATIENT REQUEST

In the course of treatment, the patient may ask the therapist to become involved in a legal matter, such as providing information for a Workers' Compensation claim or for a child custody hearing. As noted earlier, to act on such requests may be to alter the treatment relationship. Thus, a clinician in this situation may wish to suggest that an independent examination be undertaken. However, if a therapist finds it necessary to offer a forensic opinion, this new role should be formalized with the patient through a signed release, a consultation with the patient's attorney, a disclosure of what opinion will be offered, and an honest assessment of how the treatment relationship may be changed. A therapy consultant may provide insight into whether positive treatment remains possible after this shift of roles and disclosure.

SUBPOENA

Subpoenas, typically, are aimed at compelling testimony at trial. However, witnesses and records may also be subject to subpoena at the discovery stages that precede trial. Nowhere in the legal system is justification accepted for the failure to comply with the initial requirements of a subpoena—the requirement of appearance in court (or before counsel) or production of documents. A therapist or expert witness who believes a valid reason exists to withhold subpoenaed information must nonetheless respect the obligation to appear and bring the requested documents. Only at that point may the litigant's right of access to the requested information be properly adjudicated.

Two forms of subpoena are in common use: the subpoena that compels attendance by a potential witness (a simple subpoena) (see Figure 4 for an example) and the subpoena *duces tecum*, which requires the production of records (see Figures 5 and 6 for examples). Commonly, a subpoena *duces tecum* is directed to medical records librarians, superintendents, administrators, or other individuals who maintain and control medical records. The subpoena *duces tecum* is designed only to produce records, not to elicit testimony. In contrast, the simple subpoena commands a witness both to appear and to testify, frequently also commanding the witness to bring records relevant to the testimony.

The law views the therapist as a keeper of information, with

AO 89 (Rev. 5/85) Subpoena

United States District Court

DISTRICT OF

V.

SUBPOENA

CASE NUMBER:

TYPE OF CASE	SUBPOENA FOR
☐ CIVIL ☐ CRIMINAL	☐ PERSON ☐ DOCUMENT(S) or OBJECT(S)

TO:

YOU ARE HEREBY COMMANDED to appear in the United States District Court at the place, date, and time specified below to testify in the above case.

PLACE	COURTROOM
	DATE AND TIME

YOU ARE ALSO COMMANDED to bring with you the following document(s) or object(s): *

☐ *See additional information on reverse*

This subpoena shall remain in effect until you are granted leave to depart by the court or by an officer acting on behalf of the court.

U.S. MAGISTRATE OR CLERK OF COURT	DATE
(BY) DEPUTY CLERK	

This subpoena is issued upon application of the:	QUESTIONS MAY BE ADDRESSED TO:
☐ Plaintiff ☐ Defendant ☐ U.S. Attorney	ATTORNEY'S NAME, ADDRESS AND PHONE NUMBER

*If not applicable, enter "none".

Figure 4

	*	
	*	
	*	IN THE
STATE OF MARYLAND	*	MEDICAL DEPARTMENT OF THE
	*	CIRCUIT COURT FOR
vs.	*	BALTIMORE CITY
	*	
____________________	*	INDICTMENT NUMBER ______________
	*	
	*	

* * * * * * * * * * * * * * *

SUBPOENA DUCES TECUM

MR. CLERK:

Please issue Subpoena Duces Tecum for the following:

MEDICAL RECORDS LIBRARIAN

____

____

to send copies of all records pertaining to ____

____ ON ________________

to the Medical Department, Room 503 Clarence Mitchell, Jr., Court House, 100 N. Calvert St., Baltimore, Md. 21202, and furnish all medical records, including examination reports, diagnostic evaluation, and clinical history and impression, relative to the patient above referred to.

____

Nicholas P. Conti, LCSW
Deputy Director
Circuit Court for Baltimore City
Room 503 Clarence Mitchell, Jr. Court House
100 N. Calvert St.
Baltimore, Maryland 21202
(301) 396-5013

1040-10-21

Figure 5

SUBSEQUENT INJURY FUND	IN THE
v. FRANK LEE FAIR Claimant	CIRCUIT COURT
	FOR
and RUGGED ROOFERS COMPANY	BALTIMORE COUNTY
	WCC NO. A-835211
and GOODE ACCIDENT & INDEMNITY CO. Insurer	89-KL-1291

SUBPOENA

MADAM CLERK:

Please issue a Subpoena Duces Tecum to:

JONAS R. RAPPEPORT, M.D.
The Professional Arts Building
101 W. Read Street
Baltimore, Maryland 21201

To appear to testify on behalf of the Subsequent Injury Fund in the above captioned case.

PLACE: Circuit Court for Baltimore County
County Courts Building
Towson, Maryland 21204

DATE: November 21, 1991

TIME: 9:30 A.M. (and continue until completion)

Please bring with you all medical records, reports, and X-rays concerning the Claimant.

GEORGE E. BARRETT
Assistant Attorney General
Subsequent Injury Fund
P. O. Box 20206
Baltimore, Maryland 21284-0206
(301) 555-2940

Figure 6

no independent interest in the information possessed, at least insofar as disclosure to the legal process is concerned. Indeed, efforts in California and Connecticut to establish a psychiatrist's separate recognizable interest in the information in treatment records have been defeated. Thus, the mental health professional whose records are subpoenaed as testimony generally is left with two obligations: 1) to comply with the initial requirements of the subpoena to appear or produce documents at trial; and 2) to notify the individual—almost always a patient—with a stake in asserting any legal grounds to exclude subpoenaed information from trial. Some states, Illinois, for example, stipulate that the therapist has the right or obligation to assert the therapist-patient privilege on behalf of the patient, at least until such time as the patient has had the opportunity to be notified and involved in the legal proceeding.

A therapist may learn that a subpoena has been issued with the knowledge and consent of the patient. Under these circumstances, both the patient's attorney and the patient must be made aware of the content of the subpoenaed material and the patient's attorney should be advised of the responses the therapist would probably give in court if required to testify on the issues of the case. In such cases, the consent of the patient to the therapist's testimony or production of treatment records constitutes "informed consent," and the obligations of the therapist to the legal system will be satisfied.

If the therapist learns that the patient either is unaware of the subpoena of treatment records or has not consented to disclosure of the requested information, the therapist should alert the patient's attorney immediately. The patient's attorney can prepare an objection to disclosure of information if the situation warrants such action. If the patient is not a party to the litigation and, thus, has not retained an attorney, the therapist should refuse to disclose subpoenaed information at least until the court has been made aware that the information may be protected by a rule of privilege or confidentiality. Normally, a court will not order disclosure until the patient has been given a fair opportunity to object and the matter has been reviewed.

While subpoenas typically are aimed at compelling testimony

at trial, subpoenas of witnesses and records are common at the deposition stage as well. Thus, prior to court review, a therapist might be ordered to appear and furnish deposition testimony or records at an attorney's office. Under these circumstances, the same guidelines regarding notification of the patient apply, with one further addendum. Any deposition may be adjourned to obtain a court ruling on a matter of evidence. A witness may refuse to answer or produce records until a judicial order is produced. Thus, a therapist compelled to participate at the deposition stage should be aware that the court may be asked for clarification before confidential information need be surrendered to counsel. The clinician should consult an attorney for guidance when there is concern about the release of confidential information.

Legal responses to a subpoena take several legal forms. The classic approach is to file a "motion to quash." Such a motion asks the court to review the validity and authority of the subpoena, to apply any relevant rules of privilege, and to release the therapist from the obligation of the subpoena. In contrast, a "protective order" does not quash the subpoena; it limits disclosure to that which is necessary to respect the rights of the party issuing the subpoena. Thus, certain aspects of the record may be released, while other portions of the record remain protected. The court may be asked to review materials *in camera* (in private) and to exclude from the subpoena anything determined to be irrelevant to the issues of the case. Last, material technically within the subpoena's demand, but not a part of the patient's record, might be excluded by court order. For example, an order may deny access to the therapist's notes but permit access to the patient's records.

Most therapists will never become party to the legal technicalities surrounding subpoenas. Rather, they will be more concerned with the practical responses required by the subpoena: scheduling, patient consent, copies of records, retention of records, among others. The following suggestions are intended as a practical guide to the clinician.

1. While most subpoenas speak authoritatively about a date, time, and place to appear or to present records, there is

normally considerable flexibility to these matters, and it is wise to call the attorney who has issued the subpoena to schedule a specific time and date for testimony. This may save hours or days spent fruitlessly in court.

2. If records rather than testimony are subpoenaed, many states allow a sealed copy of the records to be filed with the court, to be produced at the appropriate moment. This should be undertaken only after the therapist has verified the patient's informed consent to disclosure of the records. By learning whether submission of records in this manner is acceptable, the clinician may save both time and effort.
3. Copies of the subpoenaed records and notes should be made. This protects against inadvertent loss of the records and allows the clinician to have a copy for reference during testimony. Moreover, for continuity of patient records, the therapist should retain the original records if at all possible.
4. The therapist should never alter or destroy a document that has been subpoenaed, regardless of its content or the therapist's belief in privilege. Such alteration or destruction not only can be grounds for contempt of court, but also is seen as an admission of responsibility or fault that cannot be explained away. The negative effect of such an action cannot be underestimated.

SUMMARY

So long as a subpoena can be issued in a relatively mechanical way on an attorney's own initiative or by the court clerk at an attorney's request, the subpoena will continue to be a source of aggravation and inconvenience to the incautious mental health professional. However, if the foregoing recommendations are heeded, and advice and counsel of colleagues and attorneys are sought, the subpoena should hold no great peril to the therapist.

We have discussed many of the problems of the treating clinician. The next section of this guide concerns the role of the mental health professional as a nontreating consultant to an attorney.

III

THE LAW AND THE EXPERT WITNESS AS CONSULTANT TO THE ATTORNEY

9

CONTACT WITH THE ATTORNEY

Mental health professionals and attorneys view the resolution of problems from different perspectives. Therefore, the working arrangement between them must be structured so each participant can make a distinct and constructive contribution to the resolution of the particular legal issue. Each professional must know what is expected of the other and how the task will be accomplished. These matters deserve serious consideration from the beginning of the relationship between the expert witness and the legal counsel.

TYPES OF PROFESSIONAL WITNESS

The law recognizes two types of witness: the factual witness and the expert witness. For example, in the John Hinckley case, Dr. John Hopper, the mental health professional who had treated Hinckley prior to his assault on President Reagan, acted as a factual witness. During the trial, Dr. Hopper testified only to his diagnosis and treatment of Hinckley, providing those facts gathered during the therapeutic relationship. He was not asked to render an opinion concerning the assault or the extent to which Hinckley was criminally responsible. Contrast this involvement with that of Dr. William Carpenter, who was retained by Hinckley's attorney as an expert witness. Dr. Carpenter evaluated Hinckley in order to answer specific legal questions at issue during the trial. He testified as a psychiatric expert to help the jury better understand Hinckley's mental status at the time of the assault, enabling the jury to reach an opinion about criminal responsibility.

An example outside the field is equally illustrative. An automotive engineer, standing at a busy intersection, observes an automobile accident and is identified as a witness at a subsequent judicial proceeding about the accident. He is asked only to describe what he has observed. Notwithstanding his professional credential, he is properly not asked to render an opinion about the probable condition of the vehicle at cause in the accident. Such a statement would represent expert testimony, requiring a more detailed evaluation than available through simple observation. A lay witness—a factual witness—is allowed to discuss observations. Expert testimony can be rendered only by an individual who has been retained for that particular purpose.

INITIAL CONTACT

The request for a forensic mental health evaluation may come from an attorney, a patient, or a court representative. The approach may be made by personal visit, by letter, or by telephone call. If the contact is made by an attorney, certain matters deserve investigation. For example, it is useful to know the source of referral. Selection after several colleagues have declined involvement in the case or referral from nothing more substantive than the Yellow Pages usually portends a difficult experience.

Should the patient—the attorney's client—personally call to request an evaluation for legal purposes, the clinician should insist on speaking to the attorney first before undertaking such an evaluation. By ensuring that the "contract" for evaluation is with the attorney, the clinician assures that the content of that evaluation comes under the protection of attorney-client privilege. Moreover, only through communication with the attorney can the clinician establish a clear understanding of the legal questions involved, the possible roles to be played in the judicial action, and the fee arrangements.

At the point of initial contact, the expert should learn as much as possible about the case. Is it a criminal or civil matter? Is the person to be evaluated known to the expert? What is the legal issue at the heart of the matter? The expert should learn the preliminary trial date, the date by which the report is needed, and the requirements for court testimony or depositions. The expert should make sure there is sufficient time to undertake a complete evaluation. If the report to be prepared is about a former or current patient, a number of special legal and professional questions arise that need to be explored carefully. Part II of this report discussed the role of the treating professional in the legal system at greater length.

During the initial contact, the expert should establish who has made the request for an evaluation. A court might order an examination from a mental health professional who maintains an official relationship with the court as an employee of the city, county, state, or federal government. Occasionally, both sides in a dispute may agree to an evaluation by a private expert; the court then will order the evaluation. It becomes the responsibility of the person or entity requesting the examination to obtain for the expert all necessary records, reports, and statements, and to arrange the interviews required by the expert. To the extent practicable, the expert should insist on interviewing all important persons involved whose insight or information may assist in the formulation of an expert opinion.

FEES

During the initial contact with the attorney or other party requesting the participation of an expert, it is important to discuss fees and timely payment. Although not always necessary, a written confirmation of the arrangement is advisable. Mental health professionals should remember that it is considered unethical to accept expert witness fees on a contingency basis, notwithstanding the fact that many attorneys have such contingency fee arrangements with their clients. Most expert witnesses charge more for forensic work than for therapeutic work because of the nature of forensic work. How much more appears to be related to the consultant's forensic experience and limitations imposed by governmental fee schedules (e.g., Workers' Compensation limitations). Experienced forensic psychiatrists may charge two to three times more per hour than their standard therapy rate. Moreover, charges are made for time spent to review records, to engage in conferences with the attorney or others, to undertake the examination, to write reports, and to prepare testimony. Experienced forensic experts generally recommend that a retainer be obtained from defense counsel in criminal cases and from plaintiffs' attorneys in civil cases, unless previous experience ensures confidence of payment. It is difficult to collect fees from a defendant who is in prison or from an attorney who has lost the case.

It is wise to have the attorney send appropriate materials about the case for review before reaching a decision to accept the case. The expert should be assured of payment for this case review whether or not the ultimate decision to participate is favorable. If the expert decides to accept the consultancy, he or she should forward a copy of his/her curriculum vitae and a letter documenting his/her understanding of the task and stating the agreed-upon fee schedule.

RECORDS AND OTHER MATERIALS

After agreeing to participate, the expert should receive all available materials—hospital records, legal documents, police reports, a full set of school or military records—and arrange interviews with family and others. If the attorney fails to furnish the expert with important information that later comes to light at trial, the attorney is at fault for having omitted it. If the new information might have altered the professional's opinion, such an admission must be made at trial, whether or not it is to the client's disadvantage.

BEFORE THE INTERVIEW

The examination site should be prearranged by the attorney. In civil cases, it is advisable to remind the attorney that more than one session may be necessary, and that psychological or other tests might be required. Civil plaintiffs or defendants, unless totally incapacitated, have no difficulty coming to the examiner's office, and many criminal defendants, released on bail or on their own recognizance, similarly may travel to the examiner. However, some defendants remain incarcerated and, in some instances, are so dangerous that authorities will not permit them to be brought to the mental health consultant's office.

Should the interview be conducted in a jail or correctional institution, the nature of the available interview facilities should be determined in advance, particularly since those in most jails are less than desirable. If the facilities are inadequate, the defendant's attorney may be able to obtain use of a private office, a chapel, or a library. If a mental health professional is employed at the facility, a satisfactory place to conduct an interview often can be arranged as a courtesy.

On occasion in criminal cases, counsel for the defendant will demand the opportunity to observe or even tape-record the examination. This occurs most frequently when the examination is being conducted either for the court itself or for the prosecution. For some experts, this presents no problem; for others it is objectionable on a number of grounds. For example, the presence of an attorney, even as an observer, may interfere with the spontaneity and openness of the interview process. The expert, conscious of a critical presence, may be more cautious in questioning and challenging responses. If the expert objects to the presence of opposition counsel, the attorney for whom he is consulting should be asked to try to prevent the other attorney from being present. Should the court authorize the attorney's presence anyway, the expert may either withdraw from the case or proceed with the examination while noting reservations about the presence of a third party.

THE INTERVIEW

A mental health professional who agrees to undertake an evaluation is ethically obligated to devote sufficient time to perform an adequate examination. The schedules of neither the attorney nor the clinician should require a rush. It may be necessary to allocate a number of hours, spread out over several days or weeks. A one-hour session alone may not be sufficiently productive to satisfy the evaluation needs; a single session of several hours may be unfair to the examinee, raising questions of fatigue and recall. Multiple sessions may also help check the consistency of the information presented over time. It is useful to discover whether the information is altered, added to, or even reversed as the sessions progress. Dangers arise in multiple sessions: The less experienced professional may encounter greater difficulty in maintaining the objective consulting role and slip into the role of therapist. The more experienced expert may discover major flaws in the case's medicolegal underpinnings, as discrepancies in the facts occur; this can lead to the "detective" role. Chapter 10 discusses the content of the examination in greater detail.

THE REPORT

After the examination is conducted, the expert should provide a preliminary oral report to the attorney. This serves two purposes: 1) to clarify the opinion reached; and 2) to allow the attorney to determine whether the opinion is in the client's best interests and should be written and submitted. In some jurisdictions, even if the attorney decides not to use the expert, he or she could be called to testify by the opposing side if the original counsel utilizes the testimony of another expert. The expert may need to assist the attorney to understand the results of the examination and to recognize the report's strengths and weaknesses. At the same time, the expert should be careful not to be swayed by the attorney to withhold pertinent material or to agree to a conclusion with which he or she is uncomfortable. The final report should be written only after this consultation with the attorney, since once a report is written and submitted, the law may require that it be available to opposing counsel. The form and content of that report may vary, and Chapter 11 provides a guide to that document's preparation.

AFTER THE REPORT IS COMPLETE

Following submission of a report, the expert will be apprised of the next steps. A deposition may be required; consultation on jury selection or on adverse expert witnesses may be sought; and the consultant's testimony will be scheduled. While most attorneys try to schedule the expert's appearance in court at a convenient time, courtrooms do not run on normal schedules, and testimony by the mental health expert may be delayed through no fault of the attorney. The best mechanism to avoid unnecessary cancellation of clinical practice responsibilities is to maintain close contact with the attorney's office. For example, if a trial is scheduled to start on Tuesday morning, and the expert is to testify on Thursday afternoon, check with the attorney's office on Monday. The case may have been postponed to Wednesday. If the case does start Wednesday, and the expert is needed on Friday afternoon, call Thursday to check that the Friday appearance is still anticipated. If so, then and only then should the mental health professional cancel Friday afternoon patients. Should the case be settled Friday morning, the expert reasonably should expect compensation for his Friday afternoon cancellations.

While this process appears to require extra effort, it is necessary to reduce frustration, maintain a reasonable schedule, and continue good relations with a busy and otherwise preoccupied attorney. After all, the expert may enjoy the break from routine office practice, and a good relationship produces additional referrals. Arrangements have now been made with the retaining authority to conduct the evaluation, which is discussed in the next chapter.

10
THE EXAMINATION

All mental health professionals who function in forensic roles are presumed to be competent both in the performance of a complete clinical diagnostic evaluation and in formulating pertinent dynamic interpretations. Therefore, this chapter will not describe the information sought in full clinical evaluations. Rather, it will highlight those aspects of the examination that are relevant to legal issues and will point out differences between forensic examinations and clinical evaluations.

PRELIMINARY WORK

An expert who is not the therapist and who is engaged by an attorney in a forensic role is not necessarily intended to become an advocate on behalf of the examinee. The expert must function as an independent expert without any implied loyalty to the party who has sought his or her services. The expert must be alert to the potential of transference by the examinee or countertransference by the examiner during the course of the examination. The consultant also must be alert to the danger of falling into the role of therapist.

As important as monitoring one's own behavior during the course of an examination is the importance of understanding the legal issues at hand. The character of the examination, to a varying degree, is determined by those legal issues. For example, an evaluation for testamentary capacity (ability to make a will) does not require a detailed sexual history. The examination should be tailored to the need at hand.

THE EXAMINATION

The examination actually begins when the expert secures a clear picture of the purpose of the evaluation and the legal issues involved. Before seeing the examinee, the mental health expert should obtain all available information about the individual from the engaging attorney, from documentary sources, from the individual, and from individuals able to provide relevant information, such as family members, employers and others. Such documentation includes medical and hospital records and reports from all institutions at which the examinee was a patient. Police records, school records, and employment and military information are also useful. Complete information retrieval is difficult; for example, photocopies of records may be missing pages, or handwritten records may be illegible. Nonetheless, a best effort should be made, since missing pages or illegible paragraphs may contain information critical to the evaluation. The importance of obtaining and reviewing all relevant information cannot be overestimated. Not only does it help the mental health professional obtain a clear picture of how the examinee usually functions, but also it may confirm or discredit data presented at the examination.

At the start of the examination, the expert should ensure that the examinee comprehends the purpose of the examination, is aware of the person requesting the examination, and understands to whom the examination's results will be made available. It is essential that the expert clarify his or her role for the examinee so that it is understood that the customary rules of medical confidentiality do not apply and that whatever the examinee says during the evaluation may be included in the report. In those cases in which the evaluation takes place over a period of days or weeks, the examiner regularly should reemphasize the nature of the examiner's role.

Early in the examination, the expert should ascertain whether the examinee is taking medication of any sort, whether prescribed or not. If so, the dosage, the frequency, and the time last taken should be documented. The expert should report specifically whether any currently used medication could affect the results of the examination.

The expert may wish to begin the examination with an evaluation of the examinee's current mental functioning, though the final, documented evaluation may be delayed until the end of the examination. This initial mental status evaluation is directed toward the individual's personality and psychological functioning at the time of the evaluation. In forensic evaluations, the appropriateness of affect to the content of speech and to the legal issue at hand is a most significant observation.

The areas of evaluation of the sensorium are standard: memory, cognition, comprehension, calculation ability, capacity for abstract thinking, and general knowledge. In all forensic evaluations, these features should be examined. The quality of the individual's judgment in decisions made or actions taken in response to past and present events is of particular importance.

While the protocol for a clinical mental health history is extensive, only specific elements are necessary for a thorough forensic evaluation. The degree of detail required in a given examination varies as a result of the legal issue at hand. In most cases, however, a clear framework of the past experience of the examinee is required, including educational, social, ethnic, occupational, and legal experiences.

A detailed marital history may be revealing in a wide range of cases, from disability to testamentary capacity, and may prove vital in custody and divorce actions. Indeed, the family history may also be relevant to the evaluation of the examinee's attitudes and behavior.

While little attention generally is devoted to eliciting a full medical history, in forensic evaluations the potential of previously undiagnosed conditions should be kept in mind. From time to time, cerebral atrophy, tumors, epileptiform, and other disorders are found for the first time as a result of legal actions. The examiner should not hesitate to arrange for neurologic, radiologic, and electroencephalographic studies and laboratory tests when indicated. Similarly, psychological testing should be undertaken as indicated.

DIAGNOSIS

Having assembled all the available information, the expert is confronted by two questions: 1) Is the individual suffering from a psychiatric disorder, and, if so, which disorder? and 2) What is the relationship of the psychiatric data to the legal issue?

With regard to diagnosis, the most recent edition of the *Diagnostic and Statistical Manual of Mental Disorders* (American Psychiatric Association, 1987) contains the nosology of preference, though a decision to use all five axes remains a matter of individual preference. However, the most complete diagnosis may be of greatest help to the attorney. The mental health professional functioning in a forensic role pursues the same differential diagnostic process as when in a clinical role. Alternative diagnoses are examined, and a final determination is made. A corollary diagnosis regarding personality functioning may also be made. However, remember that in forensic issues, personality diagnosis is rarely relevant and is usually a great source of distortion. The relationship between the mental capacities of the individual and the legal issue is of paramount importance.

While at times a specific diagnosis may be difficult, the determination of impairment and the degree of that impairment may be even more troublesome. In some actions, the legal standard may be well defined, as in competency to stand trial or to write a will. In other cases, specific guidelines are virtually nonexistent. In still other cases, both standards and reporting requirements are specified. For example, in evaluations that concern Workers' Compensation laws, it is necessary to report not only the nature of an injury but also whether the resulting disability is considered temporary or permanent and what percentage value may be applied to the impairment caused by the injury (see Appendix F).

MALINGERING

The expert must always remember that the information elicited from a patient or other examinee is likely to be distorted.

While this possibility of deliberate falsification occurs in routine clinical work, it is much greater in forensic situations. The examinee is embroiled in an adversary situation and, consciously or unconsciously, is likely to present information favorable to his or her position. However, allegations of malingering can seriously damage the patient's case.

Malingering has been classified into four categories: 1) simulation, in which nonexistent symptoms are feigned; 2) dissimulation, concealing existing symptoms; 3) partial malingering, where real symptoms are consciously exaggerated; and 4) false imputation, ascribing actual symptoms to a cause consciously recognized as unrelated to their origin (Resnik, 1984).

Situations in which malingering becomes an issue generally involve feigned mental illness and its signs and symptoms. Examples of situations in which malingering arises are numerous. A defendant may hope to avoid punishment by pretending to be incompetent to stand trial or to be insane at the time of the crime. Plaintiffs may feign illness to seek financial gain in malpractice suits or in disability claims. Soldiers may malinger in an effort to avoid combat; prisoners may pretend illness in order to be transferred from prison to a psychiatric hospital.

Most mental health professionals are hesitant to diagnose malingering for a number of reasons. Physicians generally assume that the doctor-patient relationship is a special one in which deception does not exist, or, if it does, it cannot be proven. Mental health professionals, practicing in a field rife with diagnostic uncertainties, have doubts about their own opinion in such cases.

The detection of malingering begins when the examiner becomes aware of inconsistencies in the information provided by the examinee. It is extremely difficult for an otherwise mentally well person to falsify a serious mental illness with all of its subtleties. The lack of internal consistency in what the examinee says and the inconsistencies in the story from session to session are significant. Behavior during the sessions may provide important clues.

In cases in which simulation is suspected, the examiner should learn whether the individual had been in contact with mentally ill persons or had access to information about a specific mental disorder. One individual, for example, had a small library of psychiatric and psychological books. Most individuals, however, do not have the detailed knowledge of the less obvious symptoms of specific mental disorders, and questions in those areas may well prove the issue. The expert's skill in detecting malingering lies in skepticism, in interview technique, and in knowledge of collateral information.

SUBSTANCE ABUSE

The law views all substance abuse as a voluntary action and does not allow it to be considered to reduce responsibility for a crime. There are special circumstances, however, that may allow for a reduction in the seriousness of the charges if the person was so intoxicated that the necessary "intent" was not present. This is a complicated legal issue and varies from state to state. Therefore, if the mental health professional finds compelling evidence that a serious impairment of the mind was present, the referring attorney should be apprised of the issue.

SUMMARY

The mental health forensic examination can become the foundation upon which a case for a criminal defendant or civil plaintiff is built. For that reason, the examination and each of its constituent parts must be built carefully to enable the examining mental health expert to arrive at both a diagnosis and a legally appropriate opinion. Without an adequate examination and a carefully delineated diagnostic opinion, the psychiatric legal report that follows from it may be so flawed as to render it useless in court. After the examination comes the report.

REFERENCES

American Psychiatric Association. (1987) *Diagnostic and statistical manual of mental disorders* (3d ed., rev.). Washington, DC: APA.

Resnik, P.J. (1984). The detection of malingered mental illness. *Behavioral Sciences & the Law, 2*, 21–38.

11

THE EXPERT'S REPORT

The findings of the forensic evaluation by an expert witness—the psychiatric legal report—represent the bases on which the expert's opinion stands in court. Because the purpose of the report is to help resolve a legal dispute, it differs markedly from the therapist's report used for evaluation, diagnosis, and treatment of a patient. The therapist's report generally is addressed to other treating professionals who are able to draw inferences about the importance of symptoms or specific findings. The forensic report, in contrast, is addressed to a nonmedical audience—judges, lawyers, and members of a jury. No assumptions can be made about their level of understanding of mental health concepts. The expert's report differs substantially from the therapist's report; the items emphasized vary with the legal issues involved.

The forensic report may be used by the requesting attorney or the court in many ways: in defining legal strategy; in negotiating with opposing counsel; in certain court determinations such as competency to stand trial; or in developing an outline for direct or cross-examination. Therefore, it is important that the consultant's report be prepared clearly.

FORMAT FOR THE REPORT

Reports should be self-sufficient; that is, they should contain all the data necessary to support the consultant's opinion. A reader should be able to understand how the opinion was reached based on the data in the report alone. Documents critical to the opinion should be summarized briefly. While the form of the report is a matter of individual preference, logical arrangement of the report and the use of subheadings help the reader—whether witness, counsel, judge, or jury—to find specific data more easily. Regardless of the report's form, the opinion on the legal issue that is reached by the consulting therapist should stand out clearly. This chapter suggests one format the expert may adopt for a report in a criminal case. With additions mentioned near the end of the chapter, this basic format may also be adequate for most civil cases.

CONTENT

The expert's report must contain a wide range of information, written concisely, and, to repeat, written for the lay audience, not the clinical colleague. Each of the sections suggested below must meet the tests of comprehensiveness and clarity. Sections that are not relevant to the case at hand may, of course, be omitted.

Identifying Information

This section should include the name of the examinee, sex, race, marital status, the case number or other identifying data, the criminal charges (if appropriate), and the name of the individual requesting the examination.

Reason for Referral

Here, the questions asked by the referring source should be specified. The case's legal issues should be clearly stated, such as competency to manage one's affairs, psychiatric injury due to an accident, or child custody. If the examination has been conducted at court request, the questions asked should be taken verbatim from the court order. Similarly, if an attorney or other agency has referred the case, the language as stated in the referral letters should be reiterated.

Sources of Information

The number, length, and location of interviews with the examinee and relevant others should be enumerated. Any statements made by the examinee should be reviewed, as should any police or accident reports. All documents reviewed in the course of the examination should be documented in an easily readable format. Some experts summarize the relevant sources here; others summarize them in other places in the report.

Examiner Qualifications

Commonly, a curriculum vitae is appended to the final report; that fact is noted early in the report. The expert's current position, title, and professional credentials are shown after the signature at the end of the report.

Statement of Nonconfidentiality

The report should note that the examinee was informed of and understood the limits of confidentiality at the time of the interview. It should also indicate that the examinee clearly understood that a report would be prepared for use in the legal proceedings.

Psychiatric History

The nature of the case often dictates whether to begin the history with a statement of the individual's present problem or with a chronology leading to the present problem. For example, the latter approach would be more appropriate in a case of alleged psychiatric illness following an accident; the former would govern a competency case. Under either circumstance, the history should include a full description of the problem and those factors that may have had an impact on it.

Nature of the Problem. It is important to state the reason an individual gives for being the subject of an evaluation when first queried by the consultant therapist, even if the response to the question was: "My lawyer said I should talk to you," or, "The court ordered me to see you." If a mental problem is reported, it should be stated in the exact words of the examinee.

History of Present Problem. The history takes the form of a narrative, describing the genesis and course of the problem, and indicating the relationship between the legal issue and the emergence of any symptoms or deviations in behavior. If, for example, the legal question pertains to criminal behavior and mental illness, the mental health professional should note the etiology of the disorder, the first manifestation of symptoms, the patterns of recurrence and remission, the treatment, and the response to treatment.

Subject's Account of the Situation. This section allows the consultant to quote the examinee directly. The description of the event and even the phrasing used by the examinee are usually significant. A subject might have stated to the examiner: "They say I killed my wife, and I might have, but my last recollection is looking at the drawer with the gun in it," or, "I killed my girlfriend, shot myself, and the next thing I knew, I woke up in a hospital." The examiner should note whether a statement was made to the police and, if so, how the subject's statement at that time fit with the account on examination. In criminal cases, a first-person description of the subject's prior relationship with the victim may be important. Similarly, a personal comment about any weapon involved can help clarify the extent to which the subject was "prepared for action" at the time of the crime. The use of alcohol or drugs prior to the accident or crime may also be relevant. Thus, a great deal of data reflecting the subject's condition at the time of the incident can be obtained from the examinee's first-person account.

Witnesses' Accounts of the Crime. Corroboration of an examinee's account of an incident by outside observers or witnesses is a particularly important component of the forensic report. The subject's account portrays the situation largely as seen through the subject's eyes, but does not tease out distortions, omissions, and inconsistencies. Interviews with witnesses and reviews of witnesses' prior statements may bring discrepancies to light. The expert should explain how the accounts of witnesses have been considered in the evaluation of the examinee.

Personal History and Family History. The personal and family history consists of a chronological account of the individual's life, centering on major life events—education, occupation, and military history, among others—and placing emphasis on behavior patterns at each point. The examinee's sexual history may be discussed in this section or in a separate section, based on whether the issues raised are salient in the case. The family history should relate interpersonal relationships, socioeconomic status, ethnic background, and religious customs, again in the context of emotions and behavior patterns. Marital history, included here or elsewhere, may be an important source of stress in both civil and criminal issues.

Medical History. The past or present existence of any medical illnesses should be noted carefully. Any special physical examinations or tests that were ordered as a part of the evaluation should be detailed. Instances of use or abuse of drugs or alcohol should be noted, with particular attention to use at the time of the incident.

Criminal Record. A detailed past legal history should include both juvenile and adult arrests and the resolution of those legal issues.

Mental Status Examination

This part of the evaluation is based on standard clinical observations. The text should provide both direct descriptions of the examinee's behavior and direct quotes of his or her statements. The expert should distinguish clearly between the process of description or observation and the inferences that may be drawn therefrom. For example, an examinee, relating the shooting death of his girlfriend, cries and, at times, sobs uncontrollably. However, unless the examinee actually tells the examiner why he is crying, the examiner may not suggest that the behavior is "because he is guilty and remorseful over the shooting." That would be making an inference. Many experts limit this section of their report to observation. Inference or interpretation of observations are then placed in a conclusion, opinion, or discussion section.

It is assumed that during the interviews, the expert will inquire specifically about related medicolegal areas. However, unless requested by the retaining attorney, these issues should not be raised in the report. For example, if, when performing an evaluation for criminal responsibility, the expert observes that the defendant may not be competent to stand trial, the defendant's attorney should be informed of the need for a competency examination.

Psychological Tests

A summary of any test results should be reported in terms that are clear to the lay audience. The complete test report should be appended to the report.

Physical and Neurological Examinations

Any pertinent, positive findings of physical or neurological examinations should be noted in this section of the report, again, in language that is clear to those outside the medical profession. At the same time, relevant laboratory reports, X-rays, EEG studies, and other test reports should be noted. The expert should describe the full extent of the examination clearly, including whether specific tests have been omitted or why other tests were undertaken.

Psychiatric Diagnosis

The actual diagnosis is critical, since ultimately, all forensic reports are addressed to specific legal tests that depend upon the presence of a mental or emotional disorder or of mental retardation. The diagnosis and state of mind, both at the time of the examination and at the time of the incident in question, are important. The diagnosis should be rendered in the nomenclature contained in the latest edition of the *Diagnostic and Statistical Manual of Mental Disorders*. The expert should be certain that all DSM criteria for the diagnosis are identified clearly in the report, and that those applicable in the particular case are indicated. If diagnoses that are not within the DSM nomenclature are used, an explanation should be given. Where a question has arisen about the diagnosis, the conscientious expert will add a paragraph discussing how the findings justify the diagnosis chosen and discount other diagnoses.

Forensic Opinion

The most critical part of the report is the deductive reasoning articulated in the opinion section. The weight accorded to the report is directly proportional to the strength of reasoning that supports the expert's opinions. The opinions should be based solely on the material contained in the report, including summaries of collateral data. Specific references to other sections of the report should be made to support the forensic opinion. Inferences or theoretical constructs should be distinguished clearly from factual data. The reasoning processes should be made explicit and be stated clearly and fully; the reader should not have to make inferences to understand the logic.

Conclusory judgments about a subject's behavior patterns, maturity, or impulse control should not be made unless supported by numerous examples. Psychodynamic formulations generally are not helpful, except where they can be related directly to the facts of the case and the legal issues involved. On occasion, psychodynamic opinion is the only approach to the case. A judicious psychodynamic explanation may be indicated, for example, in a sentencing evaluation.

Where there has been an allegation of personal injury, it would be important to note the course of the illness from the time of the injury to the time of the examination. In addition, the report should contain recommendations for treatment, including an estimate of the total cost of an appropriate course of treatment. Finally, an opinion about prognosis is important. In Workers' Compensation cases, information about the degree of impairment and permanence is needed (see Appendix F).

The opinion itself should be stated in the exact language of the legal standard in the jurisdiction involved. The opinion should be stated with "reasonable medical certainty" unless the examiner finds it impossible to form an opinion. If, in a criminal case, there is more than one charge, the examiner should separate the charges, reviewing each one independent of the others. The findings should be described in the language of the rule and not simply state, for example, that the defendant was "sane" or "insane."

Every effort should be made to avoid bias or the appearance of bias. It is useful for the expert to specify those factors that operate against the opinion, clarifying for the reader that all issues were considered and rejected. The report's limitations also should be specified. These limitations may include limited source material or incomplete examinations. By including statements about what has not been accomplished in the evaluation and about what factors have contributed to the formulation of the opinion, the expert may limit attacks on the report's credibility.

WRITING STYLE

The report should be framed in as objective a manner as possible. One technique is to segregate factual data from professional opinion, inference, and conclusion. The sense of objectivity is conveyed in a number of other ways. Wherever possible, the expert should avoid use of the first person. Equally, terms such as "obviously" and "it is clear," or, at the other extreme, "possibly" and "perhaps" should be avoided.

The expert should avoid appearing to be an advocate for the client. Neutral phrases, such as "the subject states" are preferable to the alternatives "the subject alleges" or "the subject claims." At the same time, the expert should not use professional jargon or technical terminology. Necessary technical terms should be defined, since the judge or jury will simply stop listening to a statement that is not readily understood.

Finally, the report is written by a mental health practitioner, an expert in human behavior, and, if a psychiatrist, also an expert in medicine. Mental health practitioners should avoid recitation of case law or detailed legal analyses. These should be left to the lawyers and the judges.

PRACTICAL CONSIDERATIONS

As pointed out in the previous sections, the expert's report is a complex document. It requires careful thought and editing in its preparation to ensure that it says what is intended to be said. For these reasons, it is often helpful to prepare an outline from which to write or dictate. Considerable editing may be necessary before a final draft may be submitted.

Whether or not the requesting attorney desires a written report, the expert should dictate or outline a report for the files while memory of the examination is still fresh.

On occasion, attorneys will request preliminary reports. These should be undertaken with caution, since they are furnished before all the data have been obtained and evaluated. Such reports should be labeled clearly as preliminary; findings should be based only on the data at hand.

SUMMARY

Forensic reports should be realistic as well as objective. The quality of one's thinking as a practitioner is reflected in the report. A precise, lucid document conveys a sense of clear thinking and increases the likelihood that it will be used. A diffuse, vague report suggests fuzzy thinking and is easily discounted. The report is written. Now it is time to be deposed or to testify.

12

PREPARING FOR DEPOSITION OR TRIAL

After evaluating an individual and sending a written report of the findings to the requesting party, the expert may be expected to appear in court or to render a deposition. In some cases, the attorney may have used the report in a plea bargain or negotiation, settled the case, and avoided a trial. In other instances, the expert's report may be introduced as evidence, and the expert will not need to appear in court. The latter frequently occurs in competency determinations, in juvenile court sessions, or in administrative legal situations such as Workers' Compensation claims, parole hearings, or Social Security disability insurance adjudication. Yet, on occasion, the expert will need to render a deposition or appear in court.

At trial, the expert is required to appear primarily to enable opposing counsel the opportunity for cross-examination. As protected by the Constitution, the criminal defendant has the right to confront his or her accusers and, by extension, their witnesses. To that end the witnesses must be present in court. At a more practical level, the expert may be called to trial because the retaining attorney believes the judge or jury will be impressed favorably by the expert. If the attorney considers the expert to be a strong witness for the attorney's position, the expert can expect to be called.

PERSONAL PREPARATION

Preparation for court testimony or for rendering a deposition is similar to the preparation that precedes an oral examination. The first step is to review all pertinent records and notes, to confirm the logic of one's reasoning in light of alternative diagnoses, and to detect the strengths and weaknesses of the argument (Sadoff, 1988). The expert witness should reread, in detail, all medical or hospital records to know what material is contained in the nursing notes, the medication report, and the doctors' orders. It is important to distinguish between information provided by the examinee and that gathered from other sources such as spouse, police reports, confession, or physician's office notes. In some jurisdictions, information from external sources may be considered hearsay and, therefore, not admissible unless presented by the source.

If six months or more have transpired since the last examination, the expert witness should consider the advisability of a reexamination. Not infrequently, the retaining attorney will suggest such a course of action to ensure that current information is available. The expert whose prognosis is based on old information will be open to criticism from opposing counsel unless the examinee's present condition and degree of disability are also known. Indeed, if reexamination discloses considerable improvement, the legal strategy may be altered.

The expert witness should be prepared to explain the nature of the consultation examination and how an interview is conducted, why psychological tests were or were not ordered, and why neurological referral was or was not undertaken. Reliance upon test reports performed by professionals not known to the expert witness must also be justified.

If appropriate, the expert witness should review testimony he or she has presented in similar cases. Previous deposition testimony in the current case should be reviewed to avoid potential inconsistencies. If an opinion has changed since deposition, possibly due to new information, the expert witness should be prepared to explain the change. The expert witness should review the pertinent medical literature as well (e.g., Gutheil & Applebaum, 1982). Attorneys who specialize in medical litigation may be highly knowledgeable. The expert witness should assume that any good trial attorney owns a copy of the latest *Diagnostic and Statistical Manual of Mental Disorders*, (American Psychiatric Association, 1987) and may use it in cross-examination. Thus, it is important to be conversant with the diagnostic criteria for the diagnosis selected. Any of the expert's personal publications that are relevant to the case should be reviewed, since the opposing attorney probably also has read the publications.

All this may seem formidable and time consuming, but it will assist in maintaining poise in the unfamiliar courtroom environment. The cross-examining attorney, although generally knowledgeable, remains a mental health amateur. Cross-examination is rarely overwhelming to the well-prepared witness.

PREDEPOSITION OR PRETRIAL CONFERENCE

The importance of a pretrial or predeposition conference with an attorney cannot be overestimated. This mutual educational process can identify problems and potential misunderstanding, can clarify differences in concepts and vocabulary, and can promote mutual ease and confidence (Halleck, 1980).

From the attorney, the expert witness can learn much to facilitate comfort on the witness stand. The attorney may have information from the deposition of opposing witnesses, perhaps including that of an opposing expert witness. The attorney may have deposed a therapist and may have learned something that either will corroborate the expert's opinion or will necessitate change or explanation. Thus, each of the legal issues should be reconsidered in light of any new data.

In conference, the expert may learn that some of the information about the client is legally inadmissible at trial, such as prior convictions, present insurance coverage, and malpractice claims against a doctor. The determination of admissibility of any information rests with the court. The attorney may inform the expert witness that he or she has conferred with the court and that prior information, such as that mentioned above, has been agreed to be irrelevant to the case at hand. Thus, the expert witness should not mention such information at trial.

Alternatively, the attorney may ask the expert to omit certain data because they do not mesh with trial strategy. Negotiation may be necessary, particularly if the expert believes that the disputed material supports the psychiatric or psychological conclusions. Ethical considerations will have to determine whether it is reasonable to omit certain data on direct examination. No one has a simple answer to the question: Is it the expert's duty to bring out data in testimony that will harm the side for which he or she is testifying, or is that the responsibility of the cross-examiner? The expert may find it useful to remind the attorney that, while facts or opinions may be omitted from testimony, they cannot be erased from the mind. If asked about such data during cross-examination, the expert will be obliged to reveal them.

During the conference, the attorney briefs the expert about the opposing counsel's style of cross-examination. For example, the retaining attorney may suggest, "Opposing Attorney B is affable and pleasant, but don't be deceived. She is sharp and will ask straight, simple questions with obvious answers, then throw a curve." Or, "Opposing Attorney G is apt to bear down, be sarcastic, question your ability, and try to provoke you to argue with him. His idea is to show the jury you are a biased advocate. Keep your professional cool and answer reasonably. If he gets too rough, I will object and protect you." The attorney also should review the probable direction of the cross-examination—what the opposing counsel will try to prove or disprove, and what possible weaknesses in the report will be stressed by opposing counsel.

In a similar vein, the attorney can inform the expert about the judge. Is he conservative or liberal? What is her attitude toward mental illness and mental health professionals? How does he deal with expert witnesses in general? This information is helpful, particularly if the trial is in federal court, where judges are permitted greater leeway to question witnesses directly.

From the expert witness, the attorney may learn of material helpful in direct examination (Curran et al., 1980). The expert should state in plain English the nature of the presenting disorder, the degree of disability, and the probable future course of the disorder. The expert witness may need to explain such terms as "dissociative reaction," "delusion," or "adjustment disorder." If test reports were relied upon in reaching clinical conclusions, the uses and presumed objectivity of the specific psychological tests should be mentioned.

The retaining counsel may ask for general information about the experts for the other side and about the meaning of opposing experts' evaluative reports. At conference, the expert witness may point out weaknesses in the opposing report, suggest ways to cross-examine the opposing expert witness, and recommend how to use differing expert opinions to advantage. Because the expert accepts the additional roles of consultant and tactician, it is acceptable to discuss known professional strengths or weaknesses of a colleague on the opposite side. While discomforting to the colleague, this kind of help may clarify the clinical issues, defend the expert's own position, and discharge an obligation to the examinee and the attorney. Of course, common gossip has no place here.

DEPOSITIONS

In a deposition, a witness is asked a series of oral questions by the opposing attorney and answers the questions to the best of his or her ability. Depositions take place prior to the actual conduct of the trial, but are not simply a rehearsal. In up to 90% of civil cases, the matter is settled following depositions of the plaintiff, defendant, experts, witnesses, and other lay persons. Frequently, no report will be requested of the expert, so that the other side's first view of the expert's opinion will come from the deposition. Therefore, it is imperative that the expert witness be as well prepared for a deposition as for a trial. All hospital and other appropriate records, including other depositions that already may have been taken, should be reviewed in detail. Appropriate literature or other data supporting the expert's view must be scrutinized and be made available. While the deposition is not a mini trial, since it lacks the formal stages through which a trial passes—direct examination followed by cross-examination, etc.—it has become the most important means through which each side may determine the strengths of its case.

At the beginning, a qualified court reporter, present to record the proceedings, administers the standard oath for the witness to tell the truth. A deposition may be taken in the expert witness's office, if it can accommodate the court reporter and two or three attorneys. It may be more convenient for the deposition to be held in the attorney's offices. Although the atmosphere may be deceptively informal, every word said has the same weight as if it were said in the courtroom. Prior to a deposition, the expert should have a commitment from the deposing attorney regarding the amount of time required, the expert's fee, and the attorney's plan of payment. Most depositions last three to four hours. Generally, the deposing attorney pays the expert when the deposition is completed.

There are two types of deposition—discovery and testimonial—differing widely in their purpose. The first and most frequent type attempts to discover the content of the testimony that will be presented at trial. The second type of deposition records a transcript of testimony for actual presentation at trial when a personal appearance is not possible. In the latter case, the retaining attorney generally requests the deposition. For example, if the trial is to be held in a distant city, or if the expert will be unable to attend the trial, the attorney may settle for a transcript of the deposition to be read to the jury at trial. Some attorneys videotape the deposition and show the tape later in court. This makes the presentation more lively and personalized than would have been the case had the transcript been read verbatim.

The deposition is used more frequently by opposing counsel to discover what the witness would say at trial. That is why it is called a "discovery deposition." One goal is simply to size up the expert witness. A second purpose is to force the expert to commit to opinions and conclusions (called "freezing the testimony") in the usually relaxed, even friendly atmosphere of the deposition. The opposing counsel can study the deposition transcript, share it with his or her own expert witness, and prepare vigorous cross-examination for trial. If the expert's trial testimony differs from the deposition, the discrepancy can be used to embarrass or to cast doubt on the veracity of the witness. A further aim of this type of deposition is to uncover facts in the other attorney's case. After a discovery deposition, on occasion, an attorney is so impressed with his opponent's case or by the superior performance of the witness, that the case is settled prior to trial.

Both types of deposition (discovery and testimonial) differ from a trial in several respects. In depositions, no judge, jury, or audience is present, though the litigant may choose to attend. When the opposing attorney requests a deposition, he or she does most of the questioning; the retaining attorney usually elects to say little. The retaining attorney is there to protect the interests of both the client and the expert witness. On occasion, the retaining attorney may object to a question to prevent the expert from being badgered and even may instruct the expert not to answer a particular question.

In a deposition, the opposing attorney may ask questions of a broad or leading nature, which would not be permissible in court. In such an instance, the retaining attorney would probably enter an objection for the record. The witness would be obliged to answer unless the retaining attorney instructed otherwise. Attorneys customarily avoid an argumentative posture in a deposition. At times, however, the proceedings may be adjourned until a judge's ruling on the admissibility of a question can be obtained.

Since this is the first time opposing counsel has the opportunity to explore the nature and extent of the expert's opinion, the deposition may last for an entire day or several days. The initial part of the questioning usually will review the expert's background and focus in great detail on the amount of training and experience the expert has had in the specific area of the case in question (for example, if the amount of medication a patient was given is felt to be inappropriate, the expert's training, knowledge and frequency of experience with the medication will be explored at length). In addition, if the expert has testified previously, the details of each case and the side on which the expert has testified may be explored in an attempt to expose any potential bias.

Recently, opposing attorneys have asked experts about their income, any malpractice suits, marital status, and whether they passed their boards the first time, and so on. While the expert does not have to answer a truly objectionable question, these questions do underscore the reliability and qualifications of the expert, and must be answered. While a deposition allows broader questioning than a trial, similar questions are now being admitted at trial.

Any notes that were made during the review of records, as well as any literature on which the expert relied in support of his or her opinion, may be requested. Citations or actual copies of articles may be requested.

The attorney will attempt to determine the scope and limits of the expert's opinion in the specific case. This is done to define the case so that few surprises will occur if the case goes to trial. Unlike criminal cases, the expectation here is that both sides are fully aware of the evidence and opinions prior to trial. The expert generally will *not* be allowed to testify to any additional claims or conclusions if the opposing side has not been given notice and an opportunity to depose the witness prior to trial.

If the expert believes that a line of questioning is problematic, it is appropriate to ask for a break for a few minutes to confer with counsel "off the record." Frequently, the expert will be asked to show where in the record a specific statement came from. Since it is not possible to anticipate all such questions, the expert should feel free to take whatever time is necessary to find the statement, even if it requires 10 to 20 minutes. It should be clear that thorough preparation for a deposition is necessary.

As when testifying at a deposition or a trial (see Chapter 13), the expert witness should not answer a question unless it is clearly understood. Clarification should be sought, and then the answer should be framed as concisely as possible. Information suggested by the tenor of the question, though generally relevant, should not be offered. If counsel fails to ask the expert witness to provide all relevant information, it should not be volunteered since it may only serve as further ammunition for the opposing attorney.

At the end of the deposition, the expert will be asked either to read and sign a copy of the transcript or to waive signature. It is advisable to read the transcript to correct spelling and punctuation. The deposed expert cannot change the text, but if a transcription error has been made, the expert can note this for clarification. The transcript also allows the expert to refresh his or her memory in preparation for trial.

JURY SELECTION

Many trial attorneys try to select jurors who will be favorable to their clients or, at least, not prejudiced against them. In the jury selection process, if cause if found, each attorney may reject prospective jurors. The court process also allows a number of arbitrary dismissals, requiring no explanation to the court. The attorneys may seek advice from the expert witness about the kinds of jurors to select for the most favorable response to the client. The expert may have ideas about the personal characteristics of potential jurors that may affect their view of the client, such as age, education, occupation, social class, or religion. For example, in a case involving a 20-year-old drug addict who robbed a filling station, the expert might advise the selection of young jurors likely to identify with the defendant. Some question the value of such clinical input. Several books about jury selection are available (Hans & Vidmar, 1986; Wishman, 1986).

SUMMARY

By working with the retaining attorney, both at deposition and in pretrial preparation, the expert witness may learn and impart much about the case and its conduct prior to trial. The time leading to trial is one in which the expert must be particularly clear in his role, treading the thin line between consultant and advocate. It is also at this time that the expert's efficacy of style and of opinion are put to their most strenuous test before the court appearance. The work is among the most demanding and labor intensive of any activity in which a mental health professional may engage.

Now that the pretrial conference and deposition have been accomplished, we are ready to look at the problems of the expert witness when called upon to testify in court.

REFERENCES

American Psychiatric Association. (1987). *Diagnostic and statistical manual of psychiatric disorders* (3rd ed., rev.). Washington, DC: APA.

Curran, W.J., McGarry, A.L., & Petty, C.S. (1980). *Modern legal medicine, psychiatry and forensic science*. Philadelphia: F.A. Davis.

Gutheil, T., & Applebaum, P. (1982). *Clinical handbook of psychiatry and law*. New York: McGraw-Hill.

Halleck, S. (1980). *Law in the practice of psychiatry*. New York: Plenum Press.

Hans, V.P., & Vidmar, N. (1986). *Judging the jury*. New York: Plenum Press.

Sadoff, R. (1988). *Forensic Psychiatry* (2nd ed.). Springfield, IL: Charles C Thomas.

Wishman, S. (1986). *The anatomy of a jury: The system on trial*. New York: Times Books.

13
COURT TESTIMONY

The objective of a trial is the peaceable settlement of a dispute with the appearance of fairness. Trials make no pretense of being scientific. Cast into the midst of the legal battle, known in the US as the adversarial system of jurisprudence, the ethical mental health witness must resist the temptation to assume an advocate's role (Curran et al., 1980).

The "expert" witness is an "opinion" witness, who contributes to factual determinations in both civil and criminal cases by providing advice and testimony on matters not within common knowledge. Ordinarily, witnesses may not offer opinions during testimony. The jury, a group of ordinary people, is supposed to hear the factual evidence and form its own collective opinion. Yet, the judicial process recognizes the need for expert assistance in areas in which ordinary understanding and judgment do not permit jury members to draw inferences and to form opinions. The use of expert testimony, however, is accompanied by a number of safeguards.

To testify, the mental health expert must be able to give an opinion at the level of "reasonable medical certainty/probability." Because expert testimony represents an informed opinion based on the art and insight of the clinician and not based on scientific fact or certainty, the reasonable medical certainty/probability standard generally is considered as "more probable than not." The law is not interested in speculation, nor does it wish to hear theories not shared by at least a sizable cohort.

A second, frequently invoked protection prohibits the expert from offering an opinion on the "ultimate issue." The expert should not be permitted to influence the jury unduly by stating a conclusion on issues central to the proceedings. It is feared that the jury may give undue weight to the expert's opinion on the ultimate question and substitute the expert's opinion for their own. This protection is frequently difficult to apply in practice. For example, in criminal matters in some jurisdictions, the expert witness may not opine that the defendant is incompetent to stand trial. The expert must say that the defendant can neither understand the nature of the proceedings nor assist counsel in the preparation of his defense. In child custody cases, some courts limit expert opinion to an assessment of the parenting capacities and do not let the expert offer an opinion as to who should receive custody. While the bias of the judicial process is to steer expert testimony away from the ultimate issue, judges and attorneys are tempted, just the same, to ask for the expert's comments.

A third common safeguard requires the expert to offer an opinion in response to a hypothetical question, based on specific evidence presented in the case.

One should never assume that an expert witness can be completely impartial. Whether employed by the court or by an attorney, the expert witness initially adopts an impartial attitude. However, once an opinion has been formed, the expert witness often identifies with that opinion and hopes for the success of the side that supports his opinion (Diamond, 1959). When the mental health professional takes the witness stand, an effort must be made to preserve both truth and professional integrity. When testifying, the expert must guard against any sense of loyalty to the retaining attorney that would cause a shift in thinking from that of an objective expert witness to that of an advocate. Moreover, the expert witness must not go beyond the available data and the scholarly foundation of the testimony (Brodsky & Poythress, 1985). Blatant advocacy is recognized easily, diminishing the credibility of the expert witness.

OVERVIEW OF COURT TESTIMONY

In court, an expert witness first undergoes direct examination by the attorney who called him or her to testify. Nonleading questions are posed that allow the witness to express opinions and reasoning without interference. Cross-examination, conducted by the adversary attorney, then tests the credibility of the testimony. Redirect examination—sometimes called rehabilitation—allows the retaining attorney to repair damage and to clarify points from cross-examination. Re-cross-examination by opposing counsel must be limited to issues raised in the redirect examination.

A number of rights are accorded the expert witness in court (Danner, 1983). If the expert has a question about how or whether to answer a question, the judge's counsel may be sought. The judge may also be asked whether material sought by opposing counsel may be protected under either attorney-client privilege or therapist-patient privilege. In almost all situations, the role of the judge is to rule on legal issues, the rules of law. This may include such issues as the admissibility of certain evidence, whether a witness qualifies as an expert, whether to sustain or overrule an objection by one of the attorneys. In addition, when the judge sits alone (i.e., without a jury), he or she also is the trier of the facts, the final decision maker. In a criminal case, the judge decides whether the State has met its burden of proving that the defendant committed the crime beyond a reasonable doubt. However, when the judge sits with a jury, he or she may rule only on the legal issues and may not usurp the province of the jury by allowing the jurors to know his or her evaluation of the facts. It is the jury's duty to determine the factual issues, unfettered by the judge's opinion.

The expert witness is permitted to refer to written records to refresh recollection of a specific fact or event. The expert may state that he or she does not know an answer to a question, may ask for clarification or repetition of unclear questions, and may refuse to respond to queries that are not understood.

When simple affirmative or negative responses are requested, the expert witness may receive the judge's permission to qualify the answer further. When responding to a question, the expert witness has the right to complete the answer and may protest interruptions.

DIRECT EXAMINATION

While the content of testimony should be the focus of attention during a witness's presentation, other factors, beyond content, influence the impact of the testimony on the judge and jury. Foremost among them is the credibility of the expert witness. It is critical to establish the expert witness's credibility with the jury. That credibility may be divided into three areas: 1) expertise—the witness's credentials, training, and experience; 2) trustworthiness—sincerity, the appearance of objectivity, and the lack of partisanship; and 3) dynamism—the style of delivery (Bank & Poythress, 1982). The first opportunity to address these issues occurs on direct examination.

The judge and jury's initial impressions are established through the witness's dress and demeanor. Loud clothing is likely to detract from credibility. Male witnesses should wear dark suits. Solid colors enhance credibility; pinstripes confer greater authority (Malloy, 1987). Female experts appear most credible in solid-colored suits with skirts that fall below the knee. Conservative dresses with contrasting blazers are also effective (Malloy, 1987). Both male and female witnesses should avoid wearing heavy jewelry or ostentatious accessories. The expert witness's style of speech has considerable impact on credibility. In controlled studies of mock testimony, "powerful" speech was found to be more convincing than "powerless" speech (Erickson et al., 1978). Powerful speakers are straightforward and give more one-word answers than powerless speakers. The strong speaker neither hedges nor hesitates.

On direct examination, the expert's qualifications are established first. While all credentialled mental health professionals ordinarily will be recognized as expert witnesses, with the right to render opinions, credentials and honors increase the weight accorded the testimony. The listing of qualifications should include schools attended, internship and residency training (if appropriate), academic titles, hospital affiliations, organizational memberships, offices held, honors, licenses, board certifications, and work experience. Journal and book publications should be mentioned, particularly if they are relevant to the case at hand. To avoid the appearance of immodesty, the witness should have the qualifications elicited by the attorney in a series of short questions.

The expert is next asked to describe the clinical examination and the background materials reviewed in the development of the report of the examination. Following this question, the mental health expert is asked whether an opinion has been formed with reasonable medical or psychological certainty. The response should be a simple yes or no. According to courtroom ritual, the witness may not offer an opinion until asked. Only at that point may the witness explain the basis for the opinion—the underlying data and step-by-step logic used to reach the conclusion. This is the witness's opportunity to present his or her opinion most effectively. When possible, expert witnesses should make use of direct quotes from the examinee to demonstrate a point. For example, an actual description of specifically articulated delusions in the examinee's own words has substantially more impact than a clinical statement that the examinee had paranoid or grandiose delusions.

While narrative direct testimony appears to be more effective than fragmented, short answers, the witness should avoid prolonged, soporific narratives. Responses to specific questions should be relatively short, clear, and stated in simple language. Generally, the "homier" the analogy, the better. While working within these guidelines, the witness nonetheless must behave naturally. A stilted presentation may raise questions about the witness's sincerity.

Expert witnesses should not use technical jargon in court. It is likely to be misunderstood, not understood, or sound ridiculous. Many technical words are used in ordinary conversation, but may have differing meanings to the lay person. For example, to the lay person, a psychopath is a refugee from a mental hospital and therefore insane. If equivalent terminology exists—using "mood" for "affect, for example—it should be employed. Some attorneys prefer expert witnesses to use technical terms with explanations; members of this Committee believe that is best to testify in a clear understandable fashion, using as few clinical terms as possible. On occasion, the use of charts or a blackboard can help to clarify concepts. Few juries would understand the statement: "The patient showed marked psychomotor retardation and considerable inhibition of speech. Some ideas of reference were implied, although no frank delusion formation was evident." In contrast, few would fail to understand an expert's meaning of: "The patient's movements were slow and his voice was low and monotonous. He spoke little, volunteering nothing. He felt that certain people were discussing him when speaking privately, but he did not show any clear cut delusions about this—just vague ideas that he was the subject of other people's conversations" (Davidson, 1965).

Other rules of thumb for the expert witness in court suggest that humor has little place in the courtroom and that arrogance has no place at all. The expert witness should respond to questions directly and should not volunteer unsolicited information. Conclusions should be stated as professional opinions, not impressions, feelings, or speculations. Simply, the mental health professional in court should be just that—a professional.

CROSS-EXAMINATION

Types of Cross-Examiner

The expert witness should be prepared to encounter three particular types of cross-examiners (Bank & Poythress, 1982). The first is the "country lawyer," who claims to know nothing. This type of attorney stumbles over technical words and seeks to oversimplify human action, reducing the expert's explanations to meaningless gobbledygook for the jury. A good response is to "one-down" the attorney, stating, for example, "I understand what you mean about big words; I often have difficulty understanding legal terms." This gambit places the expert witness at the same level as the jury.

The second type is the "unctuous" lawyer, excessively polite, who apologizes for taking the doctor's valuable time and refers to the witness as a "man (or woman) of science." By concealing certain information, such a cross-examiner may attempt to set the expert up for a devastating blow toward the end of the testimony. Thus, it is particularly important for the witness not to lower his or her guard when the cross-examiner is particularly friendly or unusually flattering.

Finally, the "blustery" cross-examiner works toward immediate destruction of the witness's credibility. This type of attorney attempts to bully the witness by making reference to the expert's fee and the expert's loyalty to the retaining attorney. Instead of counterattacking, the expert witness should answer respectfully. The jury will identify with the attacked witness rather than the cross-examiner.

Areas of Attack

The goal of cross-examination is not to convince a witness of error, but to expose weaknesses in the testimony. The cross-examiner's attack on the expert witness may be directed toward credentials, bias, the adequacy of the clinical examination, or the validity of the witness's inferences and reasoning in reaching an opinion.

The cross-examiner may attack credentials by attempting to demonstrate the witness's lack of experience or specific expertise. A question often posed asks how frequently the expert has testified in court—a double-edged sword. If the answer supplied is a low number, the cross-examiner may imply that the witness is inexperienced, lacking in knowledge. If the witness has testified many times, the cross-examiner may try to show the expert to be a "professional witness" or "hired gun." If the cross-examiner's expert witness is board-certified, the cross-examiner will likely attempt to uncover whether the defense's witness has completed board examinations as well, and, if so, whether the exam was passed on the first sitting. This kind of attack on the witness's credibility is the attorney's duty, and should be anticipated. Clear, honest, nondefensive answers increase the appearance of sincerity. The expert witness can help further by staying within his or her field of expertise during questioning. If asked questions about psychological testing, for example, a psychiatrist should feel free to state that although trained to understand psychologists' reports, he or she is not an expert in the interpretation of specific tests.

The cross-examiner may attempt to show the witness's bias or personal interest by demonstrating that the expert has worked solely for the defense (or State) in previous cases. If this has been true, the clinician should simply state that the opportunity for his or her expert opinion has been available to either side in any given case if sought. Moreover, the expert witness should respond directly to questions about fees and pretrial conferences. Fees can be managed with a response such as, "I'm not being paid for my testimony; I am being paid for my time." The witness, similarly, should simply acknowledge without apology the fact of a pretrial conference, if one occurred.

Bias takes other forms as well. The expert witness must be careful not to formulate an opinion before all of the facts are available. Even if additional information supports the prior conclusion, a cross-examiner may attempt to attribute premature formulation of an opinion to bias.

The adequacy of the clinical examination may be attacked on the grounds of inadequate length, the absence of complete privacy, or the failure to obtain corroborating information. A cross-examiner may attempt to demean the clinical examination by asking, "Do you mean to say that all you did was talk to Mr. Smith?" The expert may respond by describing the specialized training necessary to undertake an evaluation of the mood, thought organization, and speech patterns of mentally ill persons. The routine mental status examination may be described as a series of tests to assess such items as memory, concentration, abstraction, and judgment.

The defendant's account of a crime often will conflict with other factual accounts. The cross-examiner will try to demonstrate inconsistencies between factual police accounts and the defendant's description of the crime, to make the expert appear gullible and the defendant look guilty. The best defense a mental health expert has against such arguments is to review all possible sources of information before forming an opinion.

The general validity and reliability of all clinical examinations may be attacked. Evidence of the limited reliability of psychiatric examinations has been collected by Ziskin (1988), who demonstrates that different theoretical backgrounds predispose psychiatrists to reach differing conclusions based upon the same data. The examiner's race, sex, and unconscious and conscious needs make a difference in the information elicited from a given examinee. Ziskin points out that, prior to the introduction of the third edition of the *Diagnostic and Statistical Manual of Mental Disorders*, the reliability of psychiatric diagnosis was only 60% between two examiners, and 45% among three examiners. It is now believed that with DSM-III-R, it is up to 80% for two examiners.

The expert's best answer to this line of questioning is to acknowledge the research but state confidence in his or her opinion in the particular case. Attempts to defend the mental health professions as a whole are not likely to be successful.

Above all, the expert witness should not take aggressive cross-examination personally. The more personal the attack, the more effective the expert witness has been. The following advice given to attorneys makes this point clear: "If an opposing expert has not hurt you, do not cross-examine him. If the expert witness has really hurt your position, make a frontal assault. If the witness is shaky, show off your knowledge to get him to stick to the truth. If the witness is arrogant, appear ignorant to get him to go too far. If the direct testimony is unassailable, attack the witness's credibility, fee, or background" (Morris, 1979).

While the cross-examiner attempts to diminish the witness's credibility, the witness who responds with grace under pressure may succeed in reducing the credibility of the cross-examiner. Therefore, an expert witness should never act the smart-aleck or argue with a cross-examiner. The jury ordinarily will identify with the witness, unless provoked to take the side of the cross-examiner. An expert witness cannot win an argument with the cross-examiner. At the same time, the expert witness need not be defensive or apologetic during cross-examination. If the answer to a question is not known, it should be so stated. Experts are not all-knowing and need not apologize for the absence of a quick, sanguine reply to every question.

TRICK QUESTIONS BY ATTORNEYS*

In court, a variety of "games" are played by attorneys to discredit opposing experts. More often than not, the witness becomes the pawn in the game, and, unless forewarned, may be confused or discredited by the gambit being played.

The Shell Game Question

In this ploy, the lawyer attempts to shift dates, places, or subjects without advising the witness. Unless careful, known facts contained in the witness's report or deposition may be discredited. When confronted with such a situation, the witness should request clarification of the questions, or respond to the questions, correcting any misstatements of date, time, or place by the attorney.

The Sham Question

This is a type of leading question in which the attorney suggests the answer he or she wants. Generally, it is posed as a statement in the guise of a question. For example, "You didn't see the defendant very long, did you?" The witness's reply might sug-

---

*This section is based on an article by Thomas O. Baker, "Operator's Manual for A Witness Chair—Model 1." It is used as modified with the author's permission.

gest that the defendant was seen long enough to allow performance of a thorough examination.

The Vain Caesar Question

Playing to the witness's vanity, an attorney might ask, "As director of the department of psychiatry, didn't you know that Mr. Jones, a paranoid schizophrenic, was an escape risk?" The correct response is "no," since the status as chair of the department has nothing to do with the question of known risk.

The "You Said It" Question

On occasion, attorneys intentionally or unintentionally misquote a witness's prior testimony. In either event, the witness should immediately correct the lawyer in a firm, polite manner. Questions that appear to summarize prior testimony demand response if the summary is incomplete.

The "How High Is Up" Question

These are open-ended questions or comparisons, such as "Was the examination long?" Rather than an affirmative or negative answer, the mental health expert should either ask for clarification or respond with a definitive statement: "It was one hour long."

The "Have You Stopped Beating Your Spouse" Question

This classic trick question is known to nearly everyone. In this situation, no matter how you respond, you run into trouble. What is the correct response to the inquiry: "Doctor, is it still your practice to use electroconvulsive treatments, a practice that has been criticized by most authorities in the field?" Under such a circumstance, the attorney who has retained the witness should object.

The "You Could Have Done Better" Question

In malpractice suits and Tarasoff warning cases, plaintiffs' lawyers may know that no matter how skillfully the defendant has acted, there is always room for a higher degree of skill and care. An attorney might ask, "Really, couldn't you have done a better job protecting this patient?" A response might be to suggest that appropriate precautions were taken.

The Impossible Question

Doctors and lawyers view the word "impossible" differently. Doctors think of precise rules of physical behavior. Lawyers, however, often think of how evidence may appear to the jury, as evidenced by the following: "Well, Dr. Jones, are you saying it would be impossible to foresee the dangerous conduct of your patient?" Dr. Jones replies: "Well, I don't know that I would say impossible." The lawyer responds: "Well, if it wasn't impossible, as you have just said, then please tell the jury why you failed to protect the plaintiff against the foreseeable risks of your patient." Dr. Jones could have avoided the lawyer's trick by originally answering, "I certainly don't know of any way that a doctor could have foreseen the danger; as far as I am concerned, it would be impossible."

The "Please Forget" Question

Lawyers find that if they add the phrase "if you remember" to the beginning or end of a question, the witness often will forget the subject matter of the question.

The Double Negative Question

Remember that while two negatives make a positive, they are also bound to confuse the jury. The witness should respond with a complete thought, clarifying the meaning of the question and response for the jury.

The Knowledge Question

The phrases "to your knowledge" and "as far as you know" present a special hazard when tacked onto a question. The incautious witness may respond in a manner that implies something not intended. Consider the question: "To your knowledge, did the head nurse know about the suicide precautions before the attempt?" The witness may not know, but respond "Not to my knowledge." This answer suggests that the nurse did not know rather than witness's own lack of knowledge of the fact.

The Primrose Path Question

The primrose path is a tactic in which a witness is asked whether he or she agrees with a series of carefully worded, overly broad, and oversimplified statements that, on the surface, appear undeniably true. The witness is led to voice agreement to one statement after another, until he or she is trapped into a conclusion that he or she knows is wholly inaccurate. While many lawyers will object to such questioning, the cautious witness will ask for clarification of any such "primrose path" questions.

The Silent Treatment

In this subtle form of intimidation, the lawyer, by silence, suggests that the witness should make a further answer. However, after a few minutes, if the lawyer sees that the witness is not afraid of silence, the next question will be forthcoming.

The End of the Line Question

In depositions, lawyers should properly ask whether they have obtained all of the information a witness possesses on a particular subject. The witness who would like to leave the door open to potential additional details that may be recalled later may indicate simply, "I have told you all the information I can remember at this time."

The Punch After the Bell Question

This tactic is employed by counsel to persuade a witness to drop his or her guard before the end of testimony. A lawyer might say, "I think those are all my questions; let me have a moment to review my notes." The witness should remember that testimony is not over until he or she leaves the stand.

CONTROL IN THE COURTROOM

A good cross-examiner will seek to control the witness much as a rider controls a horse. However, there are several ways in which the witness may exert some control during cross-examination. A witness may pause before answering a question, breaking the rhythm of the cross-examination and allowing time for the retaining attorney to make an objection. The witness may further disrupt the flow of a cross-examiner's attack by refusing to answer a question that includes an error of fact or by correcting any misquotations from the witness's prior testimony.

The expert witness should try to respond fully to each question on cross-examination. The cross-examining attorney's efforts to limit a response may be seen as an effort to conceal something from the jury. If badgered by the cross-examiner, the witness can turn to the judge for intercession. Since the judge has been deferred to as a protective figure, he or she may well instruct the cross-examiner to move to another subject. The relationship between the expert witness and the judge is quite important. The judge's nonverbal expressions of approval or disbelief of a witness have been shown to have a significant effect on the jury's opinion of the expert's credibility (Miller, 1983).

Finally, Brodsky (1982) suggests that the mental health expert witness should not appear vanquished if a point must be conceded. The expert should avoid both verbal and nonverbal communications of defeat.

SUMMARY

Although many mental health professionals may prefer not to testify in court, probably most will do so at least a few times during their professional careers. Those who are knowledgeable, self-assured, and enjoy "thinking on their feet" may find the match of wits quite enjoyable. Even those who do not look forward to court appearances will find that, with good preparation and cognizance of the common pitfalls, the procedure is not as upsetting as feared. Under all circumstances, the expert witness should not be cowed by the legal process. No attorney possesses greater expertise than the expert witness who has trained in the field of mental health.

REFERENCES

Baker, T.O. (1983). Operator's manual for a witness chair—model 1: The deposition chair. In D.L. Hirsch (Ed.), *The expert witness in litigation*. Milwaukee: Milwaukee Defense Research Institute.

Bank, S.C., & Poythress, N.G. (1982). The elements of persuasion in expert testimony. *Journal of Psychiatry and Law, 10*, 173–204.

Brodsky, S.L. (1982). Personal communication.

Brodsky, S.L., & Poythress, N.G. (1985). Expertise on the witness stand: A practitioner's guide. In C.P. Ewing (Ed.), *Psychology, psychiatry, and the law*. Sarasota, FL: Professional Resource Exchange.

Curran, W.J., McGarry, A.L., & Petty, C.S. (1980). *Modern legal medicine: Psychiatry and forensic science*. Philadelphia: FA Davis.

Danner, D. (1983). *Expert witness checklists*. Rochester, NY: Lawyer's Cooperative Publishing Co.

Davidson, H.A. (1965). *Forensic psychiatry* (2nd ed.). New York: Ronald Press.

Diamond, B.L. (1959). The fallacy of the impartial expert. *Archives of Criminal Psychodynamics, 3*, 221–366; also, excerpts reprinted in R. Allen, E.Z. Ferster, & J.G. Rubin (Eds.), *Readings in psychiatry and law* (rev. ed., pp. 217–223). Baltimore: Johns Hopkins University Press, 1975.

Erickson, B., Lind, E.A., Johnson, B.C., et al. (1978). Speech style and impression formation in a courtroom setting: The effects of "powerful" and "powerless" speech. *Journal of Experimental Social Psychology, 14*, 266–279.

Malloy, J.T. (1987). *New dress for success.* New York: Warner Books.
Miller, T.H. (1983). *Non-verbal communication in expert testimony. Journal Forensic Science, 28,* 522–527.
Morris, C. (1979). Personal communication.
Ziskin, J. (1988). *Coping with psychiatric and psychological testimony* (4th ed., Vols. I & II). Marina del Rey, CA: Law and Psychology Press.

EPILOGUE

The Group for the Advancement of Psychiatry Committee on Psychiatry and the Law has tried to guide the reader through the wilderness of the legal system. For most mental health professionals, engagement in the legal system is a foreign task in an equally foreign territory. Our text has pointed out pitfalls and problems, and has offered solutions to these difficulties. As the reader has discovered, forensic work represents a departure from the clinical treatment orientation of most mental health professionals. We serve as consultants to the legal system, attempting to share our knowledge of mental health and illness in order to enable those working within the legal system to find more informed answers to legal questions that touch on mental health and illness.

Confidentiality and advocacy are the two most troublesome areas of forensic work. Social and legal advocates have made inroads into the sanctity of the therapist-patient relationship. This has occurred as a result of court decisions and statutes in the area of duty to warn (prevent dangerous behavior), in mandatory child abuse reporting, and in requirements of third-party payers and peer reviewers. The increase in tort litigation in the United States has added yet another element requiring the therapist or expert witness to reveal information to a court (the public) that otherwise would have remained confidential. We have tried to expose the reader to some of the pitfalls of double agentry (therapist-expert witness); nevertheless, the pain a professional may feel when placed in an untenable legal position cannot be avoided.

The problems that surround the issue of advocacy are equally difficult. The courtroom does not permit an academic presentation. Instead, it is an adversarial arena where the "best man or woman wins." While the expert witness's testimony should be absolutely unbiased, it would be naive to believe that this ideal can be accomplished easily. Mental health professionals, of all people, should know the effects that the numerous factors involved have on the development of an opinion. Striving for objectivity and impartiality, while at the same time advocating *for your opinion*, is a difficult goal to achieve. The Committee has tried to emphasize these two difficult areas throughout this report.

In writing this guide, we wished to help mental health professionals conduct forensic evaluations in the most competent fashion. We hope this guide has helped mitigate the sense of strangeness and has given the reader a kit of expert tools and strategies to use in carrying out the task.

APPENDICES

APPENDIX A: BECOMING A FORENSIC EXPERT

While a practicing clinician may perform credibly in court with no specialized training or experience in forensics, some practitioners opt to develop further expertise in this subspecialty. This appendix provides a description of both the formal and informal training opportunities and the professional subspecialty societies through which a clinician may gain continuing education and collegial contact.

Forensic Psychiatry Fellowship Programs

Several full-time US and Canadian one-year fellowships are available for advanced training in forensic psychiatry or psychiatry and law. Today, approximately 20 centers throughout North America offer such educational opportunities. To a considerable degree, each program is distinct, reflected in both the interests and activities of the director and the nature of the program's clinical responsibilities. For example, programs based in court clinics, state hospitals, or correctional institutions will focus necessarily on both the patient populations and the forensic issues native to those settings.

A series of accreditation standards have been developed by the Accreditation Council of Fellowships in Forensic Psychiatry, a council of the American Academy of Psychiatry and the Law and the American Academy of Forensic Sciences. The standards were designed to bring both breadth of curricular exposure and uniformity of content to forensic fellowship programs, and were published in the *Bulletin of the American Academy of Psychiatry and the Law*, Vol. 10, No. 4, 1982. The council conducted its first round of evaluations in October 1989 and accredited 10 forensic fellowship programs, eight of them for five years, and two for three years. Evaluations of other programs will occur at regular yearly intervals.

Most trainees enter the fellowship directly from residency training, though occasional fellows enter as either fourth-year residents or practicing clinicians. Each must possess established skill as a general psychiatrist to qualify minimally for consideration as a fellow. Maturity of judgment and strong communication skills are highly desirable.

During the fellowship, the trainee has an opportunity to conduct forensic evaluations under the supervision of one or more experienced forensic psychiatrists. The supervisor usually reviews and discusses reports prepared by the fellow, provides critiques of testimony delivered by the trainee, and suggests readings, research projects, and future career directions that the fellow may undertake. For intense exposure to forensic psychiatry in an atmosphere both rich with knowledge and conducive to in-depth exploration, no substitute exists for the year-long fellowship.

Forensic Psychiatry Apprenticeship

Before fellowship programs became widely available, apprenticeship was the most prevalent mechanism through which specialized training and experience in forensic psychiatry or forensic psychology was gained. This option remains available for the clinician who may not be able to engage in a year-long fellowship, but who is able to work under a senior forensic mentor. As an apprentice, one attends examinations conducted by the mentor, observes testimony in court, attends lectures and seminars at the mentor's suggestion, and reads from a suggested bibliography. An apprentice may even have the good fortune to receive individual instruction and case supervision from the more experienced mentor. Informal apprenticeship continues as a legitimate method through which to acquire specialized forensic knowledge.

Forensic Psychology Training Programs

Subspecialty training in forensic clinical psychology typically takes place at the postdoctoral level, though, increasingly, postdoctoral training opportunities are becoming available. Approximately a dozen institutions or consortia offer postdoctoral programs of study and experience under a variety of degree and nondegree arrangements. Funding by the National Institute of Mental Health recently has been available for at least some of these programs. Announcements of such opportunities can be found in the monthly *American Psychologist* and American Psychological Association *Monitor*, as well as in forensic journals. At the predoctoral level, there are about 10 joint Ph.D./J.D. programs, some of which have a forensic clinical focus. A listing of these can be found in the American Psychological Association's *Graduate Study in Psychology and Related Fields*. While predoctoral internships in clinical and counseling psychology are considered general in nature, selection of an internship that includes forensic experience can be made by consulting the *Association of Psychology Internship Centers Directory*.

The American Board of Forensic Psychology requires at least 1,000 hours of direct experience over a five-year period as well as 200 hours of supervision/consultation prior to candidacy for the Diplomate. Information may be obtained from the American Board of Professional Psychology, 2100 East Broadway, Columbia, MO 65201; (314) 875-1267.

Brief Training Programs

Short-term training programs—lasting from a single day to several weeks—are offered in a variety of settings. They range from continuing education courses offered by universities, departments of mental health, or professional societies to courses that end in certification to perform specific evaluations or examinations. A three-day forensic psychiatry board review course is offered each October, preceding the annual meeting of the American Academy of Psychiatry and the Law. Brief training courses are an important adjunct to the forensic training process but do not constitute a substitute for the case supervision and extensive reading attendant to long-term training programs.

Self-Directed Reading

Not too long ago, it was possible to read all of the major works in one's proposed subspecialty area. As in many other medical subspecialties, the corpus of knowledge in forensic issues has grown too large for such a goal to be met. Today, there are so many books and journal articles of relevance to the field that no one could hope to read them all. Moreover, information relevant to the forensic clinician is spread across many books and journals spanning a variety of disciplines, crossing-indexing systems, and even spanning medical, legal, and other libraries. Here, the inexperienced clinician requires guidance from the long-term forensic expert.

Intended as a guide to help forensic fellowship program directors select books for their libraries, a subcommittee of the Accreditation Council of Forensic Fellowship Programs has produced a list of recommended texts and other volumes. The most recent version of this list, presented as Appendix C, may be of substantial benefit to those seeking self-directed study in forensics.

It is important to monitor ongoing developments in psychiatry and psychology and the law, since statute and case law change frequently. The *American Journal of Psychiatry, Hospital and Community Psychiatry*, and *Psychiatric News* are but three of the major general psychiatric publications that contain important forensic information in nearly every issue. The American Bar Association's *Mental and Physical Disability Law Reporter* is the leading source of information about recent legal developments. A number of subspecialty journals have been devoted specifically to issues in psychiatry and the law. Of these, three stand out in quality: the *Bulletin of the American Academy of Psychiatry and the Law, Behavioral Sciences and Law*, and the *Journal of Law and Psychiatry*. The *Newsletter of the American Academy of Psychiatry and the Law* contains a number of less formal articles, case summaries, and many important announcements.

Subspecialty Societies

The American Psychiatric Association (APA) provides continuing education opportunities in both general psychiatry and forensic psychiatry. Moreover, at any given time, several APA governance Task Forces, Committees, and Commissions focus on issues in psychiatry and the law. However, the clinician who wishes to develop skills as an expert witness should consider joining subspecialty societies devoted to education in forensic psychiatry and the forensic sciences. Foremost among these are the American Academy of Psychiatry and the Law (AAPL) and the American Academy of Forensic Sciences (AAFS).

AAPL was organized to further education and the exchange of ideas in those areas in which psychiatry and the law overlap. Founded in 1969, AAPL now has over 1,200 psychiatrist members. Two meetings are scheduled each year. Its annual meeting, held each October, includes four days of scientific sessions coupled with several additional days of affiliated meetings. Courses, research sessions, and presentations by distinguished guests range from the introductory level to the advanced level. A mid-year meeting, held on the Sunday preceding the American Psychiatric Association annual meeting in May, includes both a business meeting and a special lecture, generally by a recipient of an APA-AAPL award. AAPL also publishes both a journal—the *Bulletin of the American Academy of Psychiatry and the Law*—and a newsletter. Additional information about AAPL is available from its central office: 819 Park Avenue, Baltimore, MD 21201; (301) 539-0379.

The American Academy of Forensic Sciences was organized in 1948 to promote education and research in the forensic sciences. With over 2,500 members crossing a panoply of disciplines, AAFS is organized into sections—Psychiatry and Behavioral Sciences, Criminalistics, Biology, Jurisprudence, Toxicology, Pathology/Biology, among others. Each section elects its own officers and prepares its own program for the five-day scientific portion of the AAFS annual meeting. AAFS provides an opportunity for psychiatrists and others to learn of developments in other forensic science disciplines. For example, in recent years, the Psychiatry and Behavioral Sciences section has held joint sessions with other disciplines on such subjects as the medicolegal aspects of suicide, the nature and quality of mental health care in correctional institutions, and the use of expert witnesses. Further information about the AAFS is available from its central office: P.O. Box 669, Colorado Springs, CO 80901-0669; (719) 636-1100.

In addition to AAPL and AAFS, a variety of other professional organizations maintain programs and journals of interest to forensic psychiatrists, among them: the American Academy of Child and Adolescent Psychiatry, the American College of Legal Medicine, the American Society of Criminology, and the American Society of Law and Medicine.

In forensic psychology, workshops are sponsored by the American Psychology-Law Society (Division 41 of the American Psychological Association) and the American Academy of Forensic Psychology, the educational arm of the American Board of Forensic

Psychology. AP-LS publishes the journal *Law and Human Behavior*, which contains scholarly reviews and reports of empirical research. The *Bulletin of the American Academy of Forensic Psychology* provides recent developments, news, and notes. *Forensic Reports* is a practitioner-oriented journal, which includes case reports and conceptual articles. For information, contact Cathy Oslzly-41, Department of Psychology, 209 Burnett Hall, University of Nebraska-Lincoln, Lincoln, NB 68588-0308; (402) 472-3121.

Social workers may seek information about training opportunities from the National Organization of Forensic Social Work, P.O. Box 174, Milan, MI 48160; (313) 439-7960. The Academy of Forensic Social Work, Board of Certification, certifies practitioners who meet their requirements.

Summary

Forensic psychiatry, forensic psychology, and forensic social work are young subspecialties, but are growing in importance as our intertwining relationship with the legal system becomes more complex. With training, experience, and discipline, the clinician in the field of forensics may achieve considerable satisfaction from the professional skills that enable effective communication with both the clinical mental health community and the legal community alike.

APPENDIX B: FORENSIC FELLOWSHIP PROGRAMS

United States Programs

Dr. Christina Casals-Ariet
Albert Einstein College of Medicine
Department of Psychiatry
1285 Fulton Avenue
Bronx, NY 10456

Dr. Phillip J. Resnick
*Case Western Reserve University**
2040 Abington Road
Cleveland, OH 44106

Dr. Elissa Benedek
Center for Forensic Psychiatry
P.O. Box 2060
Ann Arbor, MI 48106

Dr. Thomas Gutheil
Massachusetts Mental Health Ctr.
74 Fenwood Road
Boston, MA 02115

Dr. Charles Meyer
Medical College of Georgia
818 Aumond Place East
Augusta, GA 30909

Dr. William Logan
Menninger School of Psychiatry
P.O. Box 829
Topeka, KS 66601

Dr. Jean Goodwin
Milwaukee County M.H. Complex
9455 Watertown Plank Road
Milwaukee, WI 53226

Dr. Henry Weinstein
Dr. Richard Rosner
Dr. Peter Guggenheim
*New York University Medical Center**
Department of Psychiatry
550 First Avenue
New York, NY 10016

Dr. James Cavanaugh
*Rush Presbyterian/St. Luke's Medical Center**
1753 West Congress Parkway
Chicago, IL 60612

Dr. Leslie Major
Dr. Eugene Rice
State University of New York
*Central NY Psychiatric Center**
P.O. Box 300
Marcy, NY 13403

Dr. David Sanders
*Univ. of California, San Francisco**
Drawer A
Atascadero, CA 94323

Dr. George W. Barnard
*University of Florida**
Box J-256
J H Mental Health Center
Gainesville, FL 32610

Dr. Jonas Rappeport
*Univ. of Maryland Affiliated Hospital **
Program Director,
Forensic Psychiatry Training
Room 503
Clarence Mitchell Courthouse
Baltimore, MD 21202

Dr. Peter Ash
*Univ. of Michigan Medical Center**
Child & Adolescent Psychiatr. Hosp.
Box 0706
Ann Arbor, MI 48109

---

* denotes accreditation as of 10/90
For additional information, contact the central office of the American Academy of Psychiatry and the Law, (301) 539-0379

Dr. Robert Sadoff
University of Pennsylvania
(Part-time fellowship)
Suite 326
Benjamin Fox Pavilion
Jenkinstown, PA 19046

Dr. J. Richard Ciccone
Dr. David Barry
*Univ. of Rochester School of Medicine**
Strong Memorial Hospital
300 Crittenden Blvd.
Rochester, NY 14642

Dr. Bruce Gross
Dr. Tim Botello
*USC Institute of Psychiatry, Law and Behavioral Medicine**
P.O. Box 2945
Los Angeles, CA 90051

Dr. Donald W. Morgan
*Univ. of South Carolina School of Medicine**
Department of Neuropsychiatry and Behavioral Science
P.O. Box 202
Columbia, SC 29202

Dr. Jaye Crowder
University of Texas
5323 Harry Hines Blvd.
Dallas, TX 75235

Dr. Alan R. Felthous
University of Texas Medical Branch
Dept. of Psychiatry and Behav. Sciences
Galveston, TX 77550

Dr. Lawrence Tancredi
University of Texas Medical School
Health Law Program- Room E901
School of Public Health Bldg.
1200 Herman Pressler Drive
Houston, TX 77030

Dr. Steven K. Hoge
Institute of Law, Psychiatry & Public Policy
Box 100, Blue Ridge Hospital
*Univ. of Virginia School of Law**
Charlottesville, VA 22901

Dr. Howard Zonana
*Yale University School of Medicine**
Connecticut Mental Health Center
34 Park Street
New Haven, CT 06519

Canadian Programs

Dr. Donald Milliken
Alberta Hospital Edmonton
Box 307
Edmonton, Alberta T5J 2J7

Dr. Derek Eaves
Burnaby Mental Health Building
3405 Willingdon Avenue
Burnaby, Brit. Columbia V5G 3H4

Dr. J Arboleda-Florez
Calgary General Hospital
841 Centre Avenue, East
Calgary, Alberta T2E 0A1

Dr. R. Edward Turner
University of Toronto, METFORS
Clarke Institute of Psychiatry
250 College Street
Toronto, Ontario M5T 1R8

Dr. John M.W. Bradford
University of Ottawa
Royal Ottawa Hospital
1145 Carling Avenue
Ottawa, Ontario K1Z 7K4

APPENDIX C: ACFFP-RECOMMENDED READING LIST

Books (Required by Fellowship Programs)

American Psychiatric Association (1986). *Opinions of the Ethics Committee on the principles of medical ethics*. Washington, DC: APA.

American Psychiatric Association (1988). *The principles of medical ethics with annotations especially applicable to psychiatry*. Washington, DC: APA.

Beck, A. (1985). *The potentially violent patient and the Tarasoff decision in psychiatric practice*. Washington, DC: American Psychiatric Press.

Brackel, S.J., Parry, J., & Weiner, B.A. (1985). *The mentally disabled and the law*. Chicago: American Bar Foundation.

Brooks, A. (1974). *Law, psychiatry and the mental health system*. Boston: Little, Brown.

Brooks, A. (1980). *Supplement to "Law, psychiatry and the mental health system."* Boston: Little, Brown.

Cleckly, H. (1982). *The mask of sanity*. New York: New American Library.

Engelberg, A.I. (Ed). (1988) *Guides to the evaluation of permanent impairment* (3rd ed.) Chicago: American Medical Association.

Gutheil, T.G., & Applebaum, P.S. (1982). *Clinical handbook of psychiatry and the law*. New York: McGraw Hill.

Lidz, C.W., Meisel, A., Zerubavel, M.C., Carter, M., Sestak, R.M., & Roth, L.H. (1984). *Informed consent: A study of decision making in psychiatry*. New York: Guilford Press.

Monahan, J. (1981). *Predicting violent behavior: An assessment of clinical techniques*. Beverly Hills, CA: Sage Press.

Roth, L.H. (1987). *Clinical treatment of the violent person*. New York: Guilford Press.

Schetky, D.H., & Benedek, E.P. (1980). *Child psychiatry and the law*. New York: Brunner/Mazel.

Simon, R.I. (1987). *Clinical psychiatry and the law*. Washington, DC: American Psychiatric Press.

Smith, S.M. (1975). *The battered child syndrome*. Boston: Butterworths.

Ziskin, J. (1988). *Coping with psychiatric and psychological testimony*. (4th ed., Vol. I–III). Marina del Ray, CA: Law and Psychology Press.

Books (Suggested for Fellowship Programs)

Black's law dictionary (1979). (5th ed.). St Paul, MN: West Publishing Co.

Blinder, M. (1982). *Psychiatry in the everyday practice of law*. Rochester, NY: Lawyers Coop Publishing Co.

Bromberg, W. (1979). *The use of psychiatry in the law: A clinical view of forensic psychiatry*. Westport CT, Quorum Books.

Curran, W.J., McGarry, A.L., & Petty, C.S. (1980). *Modern legal medicine, psychiatry and forensic science*. Philadelphia: FA Davis Co.

Eichelman, S., & Reid, W. (1983). *Terrorism*. Washington, DC: American Psychiatric Press.

Ewing, C.P. (1985). *Psychology, psychiatry and the law*. Sarasota, FL: Professional Resource Exchange.

Goldzband, M. (1982). *Consulting in child psychiatry*. Lexington, MA: Lexington Books.

Goodwin, J. (1988). *Sexual abuse-incest victims and their families*. Middleton, MA: PSG Publishing.

Grilliot, H.J. (1983). *Introduction to law and the legal system*. New York: Houghton-Mifflin.

Halleck, S.L. (1980). *Law in the practice of psychiatry: A handbook for clinicians*. New York: Plenum Medical Book Co.

Hazelwood, R., Dietz, P., & Burgess, A. (1983). *Autoerotic fatalities*. Lexington, MA: Lexington Books.

Hofling, C.K. (1981). *Law and ethics in the practice of psychiatry*. New York: Brunner/Mazel.

MacDonald, J.M. (1986). *The murderer and his victim*. Springfield, IL: Charles C Thomas.

Melton, G.B. (1987). *Psychological evaluations for the courts*. New York: Guilford Press.

Miller, R.D. (1987). *Involuntary civil commitment of the mentally ill in the post-reformed era*. Springfield, IL: Charles C Thomas.

Rachlin, S. (1985). *Legal encroachment on psychiatric practice*. San Francisco: Jossey-Bass.

Rada, R. (1978). *Clinical aspects of the rapist*. New York: Grune & Stratton.

Reid, W.H. (Ed.). (1978). *The psychopath: A comprehensive study of antisocial disorders and behaviors*. New York: Brunner/Mazel.

Reid, W.H., Dorr, D., Walker, J.T., & Bonner, J.W. (Eds.). (1986). *Unmasking the psychopath: Antisocial personalities and related syndromes*. New York: Norton.

Revich, E., & Schlessinger, L. (1981). *Psychopathology of homicide*. Springfield, IL: Charles C Thomas.

Rosner, R. (1982). *Critical issues in American psychiatry and the law* (Vol. I). Springfield, IL: Charles C Thomas.

Rosner, R. (1985). *Critical issues in American psychiatry and the law* (Vol. II). New York: Plenum Press.

Rosner, R., & Schwartz, H.I. (1987). *Geriatric psychiatry and the law*. New York: Plenum Press.

Sadoff R. (1988). *Forensic psychiatry* (2nd ed.). Springfield, IL: Charles C Thomas.

Sidley, N.T. (1985). *Law and ethics: A guide for the health professional*. New York: Human Sciences Press.

Simon, R. (1982). *Psychiatric intervention and malpractice.* Springfield, IL: Charles C Thomas.

Smith, J. (1986). *Medical malpractice—Psychiatric care.* New York: McGraw-Hill.

Smith, J., & Bisbing, S. (1986). *Caselaw summary and analysis—Duty to warn.* Potomac, MD: Legal Medicine Press.

Smith, J., & Bisbing, S. (1986). *Caselaw summary and analysis—Sexual exploitation.* Potomac, MD: Legal Medicine Press.

Webster, C.D., Menzies, R.J., & Jackson, M.A. (1982). *Clinical assessment before trial.* Boston: Butterworths.

Journals

The Bulletin of the American Academy of Psychiatry and the Law, published quarterly by the American Academy of Psychiatry and Law, 1211 Cathedral Street, Baltimore, MD 21201.

Behavioral Sciences and the Law, published quarterly by Van Nostrand Reinhold Company, 135 West 50 Street, New York, NY 10020.

Mental and Physical Disability Law Reporter, published bimonthly by American Bar Association (Washington), Commission on the Mentally Disabled, 1800 M Street, NW, Washington, DC 20036.

International Journal of Law and Psychiatry, published quarterly, in English, by Pergamon Press, Maxwell House, Fairview Park, Elmsford, NY 10523.

Journal of Forensic Sciences, official publication of the American Academy of Forensic Science, published yearly by Callaghan and Company, 165 North Archer Avenue, Mundelein, IL 60060.

American Journal of Law and Medicine, published quarterly by American Society of Law and Medicine and the Boston University School of Law, 765 Commonwealth Avenue, Boston, MA 02215.

Law, Medicine and Health Care, published quarterly by American Society of Law and Medicine, 765 Commonwealth Avenue, Boston, MA 02215.

The Journal of Psychiatry and Law, published quarterly by Federal Legal Publications, 157 Chambers Street, New York, NY 10007.

APPENDIX D: COMPETENCY ASSESSMENT INSTRUMENT*

Each item in the Competency Assessment Instrument is scaled from 1 to 5 ranging from "total incapacity" (1) to "no incapacity" (5). If used for outpatient or in-court screening, a substantial accumulation of scores of three (3) or lower could be regarded as grounds for inpatient observation and more intensive workup.

Score

1. Total Incapacity
2. Severely Impaired
3. Moderately Impaired
4. Mildly Impaired
5. No Impairment
6. No Data

1. Appraisal of Available Legal Defenses
2. Unmanageable Behavior
3. Quality of Relating to Attorney
4. Planning of Legal Strategy, including guilty plea to lesser charges where pertinent
5. Appraisal of Role of: defense counsel; prosecuting attorney; judge; jury; defendant; witnesses
6. Understanding of Court Procedure
7. Appreciation of Charges
8. Appreciation of Range and Nature of Possible Penalties
9. Appraisal of Likely Outcome
10. Capacity to Disclose to Attorney Available Pertinent Facts Surrounding the Offense, including the defendant's movements, timing, mental state, actions, at the time of the offense
11. Capacity to Realistically Challenge Prosecution Witnesses
12. Capacity to Testify Relevantly
13. Self-Defeating vs. Self-Serving Motivation (legal sense)

---

* From McGarry, A.L., Curran, W.J., Lipsitt, P.D., Lelos, D., et al. (1973). *Competency to stand trial and mental illness.* DHEW 73-9105. Washington, DC: Government Printing Office, pp. 98–116. The Competency Assessment Instrument was developed by Lou McGarry, David Lelos, and Paul D. Lipsitt. Reprinted with permission.

Explication

1. Appraisal of Available Legal Defenses. This item calls for an assessment of the accused's awareness of his or her possible legal defenses and how consistent these are with the reality of his particular circumstances.

Questions such as the following will yield data relevant to the scoring of this item:

> How do you think you can be defended against these charges?
> How can you explain your way out of these charges?
> What do you think your lawyer should concentrate on in order to best defend you?

2. Unmanageable Behavior. This item calls for an assessment of the appropriateness of the current motor and verbal behavior of the defendant and the degree to which this behavior would disrupt the conduct of a trial. Inappropriate or disruptive behavior must arise from a substantial degree of mental illness or mental retardation.

For this item, obviously, observations as to the patient's manifest behavior are relevant and the content of the answers to questions less relevant. Questions we have used and found useful are:

> Do you realize that you would have to control yourself in the courtroom and not interrupt the proceedings?
> When is the only time you can speak out in the courtroom?
> What do you think would happen if you spoke out or moved around in the courtroom without permission?

3. Quality of Relating to Attorney. This item calls for an assessment of the interpersonal capacity of the accused to relate to the average attorney. Involved are the ability to trust and to communicate relevantly.

The degree of trust and relevancy of communication which the defendant manifests with an examining psychiatrist is applicable here up to a point. Usually the defendant will have had at least one contact with his defense counsel and the questions we have found useful with this item are:

Do you have confidence in your lawyer?
Do you think your lawyer is trying to do a good job for you?
Do you agree with the way your lawyer has handled or plans to handle your case?

4. Planning of Legal Strategy, including guilty pleas to lesser charges where pertinent. This item calls for an assessment of the degree to which the accused can understand, participate, and cooperate with his or her counsel in planning a strategy for the defense that is consistent with the reality of the circumstances.

Most frequently, the issue here relates to plea bargaining and agreement to settle for a guilty plea to a lesser offense. Less frequently, strategic issues such as a change of venue, consideration of a plea of not guilty by reason of insanity, or the decision as to whether defendant should testify, arise and require some participation from the defendant. The essential question is whether the defendant can join with his or her attorney, even if passively, in planning (or accepting) appropriate legal strategy. Of concern here is the defendant who insists on irrational instruction to the attorney or insists on defending himself on the basis of an irrational theory of defense. Questions which have been useful on this issue are:

If your lawyer can get the district attorney to accept a guilty plea to [manslaughter] instead of trying you for [murder—use examples relevant to the actual case, e.g., trespassing in place of breaking and entry, etc.] would you agree to it?
If your lawyer decides not to have you testify, would you go along with this?
Is there anything that you disagree with in the way your lawyer is going to handle your case, and if so, what do you plan to do about it?

5. Appraisal of Role of: defense counsel; prosecuting attorney; judge; jury; defendant; witnesses. This set of items calls for a minimal understanding of the adversary process by the accused. The accused should be able to identify prosecuting attorney and prosecution witnesses as foe, defense counsel as friend, the judge as neutral, and the jury as the determiners of guilt or innocence.

For this item, a single question for each role generally suffices and that is:

> In the courtroom during a trial, what is the job of [here list each role]?

It is particularly relevant that the defendant be aware of the purposes of the prosecuting attorney.

6. Understanding Court Procedure. This item calls for an assessment of the degree to which the defendant understands the basic sequence of events in a trial and their import for him or her, for example, the different purposes of direct and cross-examination.

An understanding of the procedural niceties is not required here. Questions we have used to elicit relevant data here are:

> Who is the only one at your trial who can call on you to testify?
> After your lawyer finished asking you questions on the stand, who then can ask you questions?
> If the district attorney (prosecutor) asks you questions, what is he or she trying to accomplish?

7. Appreciation of Charges. This item calls for an assessment of the accused's understanding of the charges against him or her and, to a lesser extent, the seriousness of the charges.

What is required here should not be exaggerated. Basically, a literal knowledge of the specific charge or charges is adequate. An understanding of the seriousness of the charges is of importance here only insofar as it might contribute to a, perhaps, cavalier or indifferent cooperation by the defendant in his or her defense. For example, if a defendant views an arson as a lark and is disposed to freely admit his action, there is question as to his self-protective capacity on this item. Questions useful in eliciting data here are:

> What are you charged with?
> Is that a major or a minor charge?
> Do you think people in general would regard you with some fear on the basis of such a charge?

8. Appreciation of Range and Nature of Possible Penalties. This item calls for an assessment of the accused's concrete understanding and appreciation of the conditions and restrictions that could be imposed on him or her and their possible duration.

Here, too, a concrete, simplistic understanding suffices. Generally, if the crime is a felony, the defendant should be aware that there is at least a potential state prison sentence, even if such a sentence is unlikely in his or her circumstances. The potential sentence need not be known with precision. Of concern here is that the defendant have at least a gross understanding of what is at risk and a motivation to protect him- or herself that is consistent with the risk. Relevant questions here are:

If you are found guilty as charged, what are the possible sentences the judge could give you?
Where would you have to serve such a sentence?
If you are put on probation, what does that mean?

9. Appraisal of Likely Outcome. This item calls for an assessment of how realistically the accused perceives the likely outcome and the degree to which impaired understanding contributes to a less adequate or inadequate participation in his or her defense. Without adequate information on the part of the examiner regarding the facts and circumstances of the alleged offense, this item would be unratable.

A police arrest report and/or communication from defense counsel or district attorney as to the real facts and circumstances surrounding the alleged offense are helpful here. If a patient irrationally perceives that there is little or no peril in his position and the case against him is strong, it might follow that he would have little or no motivation to adequately protect himself. Here, also, the psychotic person who, for irrational reasons, does not accept the criminal jurisdiction of the court might not adequately protect himself. Questions were used as follows:

What do you think your chances are to be found guilty?
Does the court you are going to be tried in have authority over you?
How strong a case do they have against you?

10. Capacity to Disclose to Attorney Available Pertinent Facts Surrounding the Offense, including the defendant's movements, timing, mental state, and actions at the time of the offense. This item calls for an assessment of the accused's capacity to give a basically consistent, rational and relevant account of the motivational and external facts. Complex factors can enter into this determination. These include intelligence, memory, and honesty. The difficult area of the validity of an amnesia may be involved and may prove unresolvable for the examining clinician. It is important to be aware that there may be a disparity between what an accused is willing to share with a clinician as opposed to what he or she will share with the attorney, the latter being the more important.

It is assumed that answers to questions on this item will not be available to the prosecution for purposes of incrimination and will be limited to the narrow question of the accused's competency. Here, too, the examiner should have adequate knowledge of the facts of the alleged offense from the police arrest report or counsel in order to record a valid score. Relevant questions are:

Tell us what actually happened, what you saw and did and heard and thought before, during and after you are supposed to have committed this offense.

When and where did all this take place?

What led the police to arrest you and what did you say to them?

11. Capacity to Challenge Realistically Prosecution Witnesses. This item calls for an assessment of the accused's capacity to recognize distortions in prosecution testimony. Relevant factors include attentiveness and memory. In addition, there is an element of initiative in that, if false testimony is given, the degree of activism with which the defendant will apprise his or her attorney of inaccuracies is of importance.

The relevant considerations turn primarily on the observations of the examiner regarding the perceptual abilities of the defendant during the clinical examination rather than on the content of answers to questions. Questions we have used are:

Suppose a witness against you told a lie in the courtroom. What would you do?

Is there anybody who is likely to tell lies about you in this case? Why?

12. Capacity to Testify Relevantly. This item calls for an assessment of the accused's ability to testify with coherence, relevance, and independence of judgment.

Here again, the relevant data arise primarily from the observations of the examiner regarding the defendant's ability to communicate verbally rather than specific content in the answers to specific questions. Affective as well as thought disorder considerations are of some relevance here, for example, if the defendant is immobilized by anxiety or depression, or is manic, loose or regressed in his or her associations and response. If questions that might come up in direct and cross-examination of the defendant can be anticipated, given the facts and circumstances of the particular case, this would, of course, be helpful, but it is not essential for a valid rating on this item.

13. Self-Defeating vs. Self-Serving Motivation (Legal Sense). This item calls for an assessment of the accused's motivation to adequately protect him- or herself and appropriately utilize legal safeguards to this end. It is recognized that accused persons may appropriately be motivated to seek expiation and appropriate punishment in their trials. At issue here is the pathological seeking of punishment and the deliberate failure by the accused to avail him- or herself of appropriate legal protections. Passivity or indifference do not justify low scores on this item. Actively self-destructive manipulation of the legal process arising from mental pathology does justify low scores.

In this item the issue turns on the willingness of the accused to take advantage of the appropriate legal protections even though he or she may feel that he or she should be punished. Will the accused, in other words, play the game, taking advantage of the rules built into the system for his/her protection. Relevant questions are:

We know how badly you feel about what happened. Suppose your lawyer is successful in getting you off. Would you accept that?

Suppose the district attorney made some legal errors and your lawyer wants to appeal a guilty finding in your case. Would you accept that?

We know that you want to plead guilty to your charges, but what if your lawyer could get the district attorney to agree to a plea of guilty to a lesser charge. Would you accept that?

Clinical Examples

1. Appraisal of available legal defenses. An elderly paranoid man charged with assault and battery with a dangerous weapon (a golf club) on a neighbor, utterly denied that any attack had taken place and indicated, "The CIA had put him [i.e., the neighbor] up to it." He was unable to offer or agree to any alternative possibility of a defense. He received a score of 2, indicating severely impaired functioning and a substantial question of adequacy for this item.

A retired sailor living alone on inherited property is accused of murder. The victim was a young boy who was among a group of boys throwing stones at the defendant's house at the time of the alleged offense. The defendant reported that he had complained often to the local police about repeated harassments, but they ignored him. He further reported that he had written to the FBI, the US Attorney General, and other authorities, with no response. Although he stated that when he fired the shot, he had shot over the heads of the boys, his theory of his proper defense was that a man in this country had the "inviolable constitutional right to protect his property with a gun," and he insisted that he would instruct his attorney to proceed with a defense only on this basis. Although insisting on his theory of defense, he did agree that his intent to fire over the heads of the boys should be put in evidence, but that it was incidental to the main defense. He received a score of 3, indicating moderately impaired functioning and a question of his adequacy on this item.

A middle-aged man with a long history of criminal arrests, mostly for drunkenness, had been found guilty in lower court of four counts of larceny from his 83-year-old girl friend of a total sum exceeding $16,000. He received four sentences of two years each in the County House of Correction to be served "on and after," a total of eight years. His lawyer appealed and a new trial in the Superior Court had been scheduled. When interviewed, the defendant proved to be concrete, passive, and underresponsive. When asked the basis of his appeal, he answered several times, "I don't know, my lawyer has all the facts." When offered the speculation that the lawyer may have appealed either on a legal technicality or because the sentence was too severe, the defendant answered, "He thinks it's too long. I hope to get two or three years." Later in the interview, he stated that his girlfriend was lying and that she had given him the money to "play the horses," and that she "was there," namely, at the race track. However, he stated, "They wouldn't believe me because of my record." He received a score of 4, indicating mild incapacity and little question of adequacy on this item.

2. Unmanageable Behavior. A young, male adult, paranoid schizophrenic, on two occasions (his arraignment and an earlier competency hearing), interrupts his attorney and addresses the court in loud tones, dismissing his attorney and insisting on voicing paranoid delusions to the effect that his attorney is a part of a conspiracy by the FBI to put him in prison because he is falsely believed to be a presidential assassin. On one occasion, he struggled with court officers in an attempt to put "a petition to dismiss," which he had written, on the judge's desk. He was given a score of 2, indicating severely impaired functioning and a substantial question of adequacy on this item.

A manic defendant, although responsive to questions and in contact, is unable to remain seated for more than a few moments during an examination and moves distractedly about the room, lifting objects, pacing and rapping the walls. He received a score of 3, indicating that there is moderately impaired functioning and a question of adequacy for this item.

During the examination, a chronic schizophrenic repeatedly grimaces, raises his right hand with three fingers extended, and then places his index finger against his right temple. This recurs whether he is speaking or not. His hand is at rest only when he places it inside the belt of his pants. He was given a score of 4, indicating mildly impaired functioning and little question of adequacy on this item.

3. Quality of Relating to Attorney. A middle-aged defendant with a diagnosis of involutional paranoid state is accused of killing a childhood acquaintance of his wife. He refused to see his court-appointed attorney and insists on handling his defense himself. His theory of defense consists of a claim of self-defense in that he and the victim struggled for possession of a gun and in the struggle the victim was shot accidentally four times. "I don't trust lawyers. They're all part of the criminal system. I'm going to tell my side of the story my own way." He received a score of 2, indicating a severely impaired functioning and a substantial question of adequacy for this item.

A defendant is accused of the murder of his wife. He is cooperative with his attorney but insists, against the attorney's advice, that he will take the stand in order to tell "my side of the story." This consists of his continuing delusion that his wife has been poisoning his food and that this has resulted in his becoming impotent and "like a zombie." He received a score of 3, indicating moderately impaired functioning and a question of adequacy for this item.

A depressed 17-year-old accused of assault and battery with a dangerous weapon is asked, "Do you have a lawyer?" He answers, "No, I have a public defender." Asked, "Do you have confidence in him?" he answers, "I don't know yet. I don't think he's very interested in my case." He received a score of 4, indicating mild incapacity and little question of adequacy on this item.

4. Planning of Legal Strategy, including guilty pleas to lesser charges where pertinent. A grandiose, acute schizophrenic is accused of illegal possession of a firearm. The defense attorney confers with the lower court judge, who agrees to continue the case without a finding on the understanding that defendant would accept mental hospitalization. The defendant is willing to accept hospitalization but insists on a trial and "appeal all the way to the Supreme Court to expose the fascist state we live in. I am L-4-C." He was given a score of 2, indicating severely impaired functioning and a substantial question of adequacy for this item.

An impotent man stabs his 12-year-old daughter to death while she stands beside his bed because he "sensed evil in her that was rotting my life." He states that he would refuse to plead guilty to manslaughter if it could be arranged and insists on a trial for murder and, "No lawyer would ever talk me out of." He received a score of 3, indicating moderately impaired functioning and a question of his adequacy on this item.

A mental retardate with an IQ of 66 is accused of a homicide. He is highly suggestible and passive. His trust and dependency are easily obtained, but he is capable of little or no independence of judgment and places himself uncritically and totally in the hands of his attorney. He received a score of 4, indicating mild incapacity and little question of adequacy on this item.

5. Appraisal of Role of: defense counsel; prosecuting attorney; judge; jury; defendant; witnesses. A young adult retardate (IQ 67) was asked, "What is the job of the district attorney in court?" He answered, "He's a lawyer. Lawyers are supposed to help people." The defendant was then instructed about the actual role of the prosecutor, but on subsequent questioning it was clear that he was still unable to conceptualize the prosecutorial functions of the district attorney. He was given a score of 2, indicating that there was severely impaired functioning and a substantial question of adequacy for this sub-item.

When asked the job of defense counsel in court, a chronic paranoid schizophrenic with a fourth grade education answered, "My own lawyer is supposed to help the law." He was then asked, "And you?" to which he answered, "Yes, a little." He was given a score of 3 on the "defense attorney" sub-item indicating moderately impaired functioning and a question of adequacy.

When asked about the job of the district attorney, a poorly educated man who recently settled in Boston after an upbringing in the South, answered, "He's there to get out the truth." He was given a score of 4, indicating mildly impaired functioning, but with little question of adequacy on the "prosecuting attorney" sub-item.

6. Understanding of Court Procedure. A young adult, white, grandiose paranoid schizophrenic accused of indecent assault and battery on a minor refused counsel and insisted that he would conduct his own defense. He stated, "I will ask the question. I will call the district attorney to the stand and expose their criminal black conspiracy against me." He received a score of 2, indicating severely impaired functioning and a substantial question of adequacy of the "defendant" sub-item.

A mildly retarded adult male (IQ 66) with a prior record of misdemeanors disposed of in lower court is charged with his first felony, breaking and entry in the nighttime. He states, "The judge will ask me questions to try to find out the truth. The lawyers are there to help me. They will ask questions, too." Attempts by the interviewer to explain the role of the district attorney in cross-examination are met with partial success. The defendant subsequently states, "I understand that the district attorney asks me questions; he's trying to send me to jail." He received a score of 3, indicating moderately impaired functioning and a question of adequacy on this item.

A middle-aged man diagnosed as an inadequate personality is charged with incest. It is his first experience with criminal prosecution. He states, "I don't know anything about the law. I suppose my lawyer will take care of me. Yes, I used to watch Perry Mason." He was given a score of 4, indicating mildly impaired functioning and little question of adequacy on this item.

7. Appreciation of Charges. A 19-year-old retardate (IQ 55) is accused of statutory rape of a 12-year-old girl. When asked why the police arrested him, he smirks and waves his finger back and forth saying, "No-no." When asked how old the girl was he says, "Not know, big girl." In an effort to establish the victim's age and sexual maturity in the defendant's eyes, pictures are drawn giving the defendant a choice between side views of women with very small, medium, and large breasts. With a mischevious and naughty facial expression, he touches the picture with the very small breasts. He was given a score of 2, indicating severely impaired functioning and a substantial question of adequacy on this item.

A young adult catatonic schizophrenic is accused of arson of a church. When asked what he is accused of, he states, "Started a fire." When asked the seriousness of the charge, he answers, "No harm (moan) stone won't burn." He was given a score of 3, indicating moderately impaired functioning and a question of adequacy on this item.

A manic defendant accused of successfully forging checks in the amount of $7,500 states, "They can't touch me. Any day now I'll be on the big board at the stock exchange. I'll cover the checks." He was given a score of 4, indicating mildly impaired functioning and little question of adequacy on this item.

8. Appreciation of Range and Nature of Possible Penalties. A 19-year-old retardate (IQ 55) accused of statutory rape states, "No jail, me go home to mother." He was given a score of 2, indicating severely impaired functioning and a substantial questioning of adequacy on this item.

An elderly retired school teacher who had recently been widowed is accused of indecent assault and battery on the 7-year-old daughter of a neighbor. His diagnosis is senile dementia. He is irascible and insists that he simply "petted" the girl and that "no further prosecution is appropriate" and that there is no possibility of incarceration for such an "act" and "jail is for rapists and revolutionaries." He received a score of 3, indicating moderately impaired functioning and a question of adequacy on this item.

A paranoid young woman who blames the mother of a former

boyfriend for their breakup forces her way into the apartment of the mother. During an ensuing argument, she picks up a poker and threatens the mother. The police are called and she is physically subdued. She is accused of attempted assault and battery with a dangerous weapon, breaking and entering in the nighttime, and resisting arrest. She states, "I suppose it's possible that they could send me to jail, but it's inconceivable. I've calmed down now. I will not further dignify that woman by responding to her trumped-up charges. The burden of these proceedings rests with her." She received a score of 4, indicating mild incapacity and little question of her adequacy on this item.

A schizoid 20-year-old son of wealthy parents is accused of grand larceny from a mail order firm where he had worked as a shipping clerk. He states, "My father has hired the best lawyer in town for me. I don't have to lift a finger in there [i.e., the courtroom]. The worst I can get is probation." He was given a score of 4, indicating mild incapacity mild incapacity and little question of adequacy on this item.

10. Capacity to Disclose to Attorney Available Pertinent Facts Surrounding the Offense, including the defendant's movements, timing, mental state, and actions at the time of the offense. The alleged driver of a bank robbery get-away car is accused of armed robbery. In a high-speed chase following the robbery, an accident occurs and the defendant suffers a fractured skull and is unconscious for 12 hours. After emergency surgery for an epidural hematoma, the defendant complains of a retrograde amnesia from the time of the accident. He further asserts that he does not know his alleged confederate and states, "He must have made me drive at the point of a gun, but I don't remember." He was given a score of 2, indicating severely impaired functioning and a substantial question of adequacy on this item.

A state police sergeant, 10 years from retirement, is involved in a harrowing ghetto riot. His patrol car is surrounded by a mob which overturns the car while he is in it. He is subsequently rescued unhurt. Two weeks later, while driving home after a period of duty, he has an abrupt amnestic episode. Several hours later, he is arrested by fellow police officers in a suburban home with a stolen car outside the home and two neighbors handcuffed to a pipe. He claims an amnesia except for isolated flashbacks. "I remember a scene with two people handcuffed to a pipe. I don't remember how

I got there. The rest is blank. I last remember being on the freeway with my car." He was diagnosed hysterical neurosis, dissociative type and given a score of 3, indicating moderate incapacity and a question of adequacy on this item.

A 50-year-old catatonic schizophrenic is indicted for murder for the second time in his life. On the first occasion, he was found not guilty by reason of insanity and subsequently released. He has been hospitalized for 10 years since the second alleged murder, after having been found incompetent to stand trial. He is now in a stable remission from his illness on Thorazine, and wants to stand trial. On examination, he states, "He [the victim] was a friend. We were in the kitchen. He leaned down to pick up something. I picked up the ax and hit him. I didn't plan it. It just happened. I didn't have any feelings." He was given a score of 4, indicating mild incapacity and little question of adequacy on this item.

11. Capacity to Challenge Realistically Prosecution Witnesses. An elderly, paranoid man attacks his neighbor with a golf club. He is accused of assault and battery with a dangerous weapon. "The whole thing's a lie," he said. "If he [the neighbor] testifies, I will stand up and tell the jury that he is a CIA agent and that he is in a conspiracy against me. I will not allow him to testify." He received a score of 2, indicating severe incapacity and a substantial question of adequacy on this item.

A skid row alcoholic with organic deterioration is accused of breaking and entering, and larceny. He states, "I don't remember things too good. Let them [i.e., the prosecution witnesses] have it their way. I was drunk. I don't remember taking anything." He was given a score of 3, indicating incapacity and a question of adequacy on this item.

A mildly retarded (IQ 67) young, adult male who is passive and underresponsive, answers, "I don't know," to the question, "What would you do if a witness told a lie about you in the courtroom?" He is then advised that he could quietly get his lawyer's attention in such a situation and inform him of the lie. On subsequent questioning, he shows that he has understood and that he would tell his lawyer. He receives a score of 4, indicating mild incapacity and little question of adequacy on this item.

12. Capacity to Testify Relevantly. A 40-year-old homeless male diagnosed as a simple schizophrenic breaks into a rural food store. He eats some of the food in the store and then goes to sleep. In the morning, the proprietor finds him. He is arrested and charged with breaking and entering and larceny. On being interviewed, there are long pauses before he can answer questions, and they must be repeated gently. "I have no money . . . I was hungry . . . I was cold . . . I went to sleep." He was given a score of 2, indicating severe incapacity and a substantial question of adequacy on this item.

A 30-year-old male schizophrenic (chronic undifferentiated type) is arrested after neighbors report that he has been shooting out of his window at dogs in his back yard. He is accused of illegal possession and unlawful discharge of a firearm. He insists on being tried to "clear the record" and refuses the alternative of mental hospitalization. He states that he was trying to "scare off" the dogs and had no intention of "hitting" them. However, he continues to talk after these objective answers to questions and rambles in a loosely associated, tangential, and circumstantial manner. He resists any interruptions in his discourses but can be stopped with some effort. He received a score of 3, indicating moderate incapacity and a question of adequacy on this item.

A mildly retarded young man (IQ 60) is accused, in his terms, of "first degree murder." He is concrete in his answers and has a very limited vocabulary. When pressed to elaborate on his answers or when vocabulary is used that he does not understand, he retreats to, "I don't know." He can, given his limitations, nevertheless, give an accurate and consistent, if simplistic, story of the events surrounding the alleged offense. He was given a score of 4, indicating mild incapacity and little question of adequacy on this item.

13. Self-Defeating vs. Self-Serving Motivation (legal sense). A 33-year-old paranoid schizophrenic is accused of murder. He is convinced that he will and should be executed since his is "the second messianic crucifixion." He declines a negotiated plea of manslaughter and attempts to instruct his attorney not to call any defense witnesses. He intends to address the court to request the death sentence since he "owes this to sinning mankind." He receives a score of 2, indicating severely impaired functioning and a substantial question of adequacy for this item.

A middle-aged unemployed house painter is accused of the murder of his 18-year-old daughter. At the time of the homicide, the defendant was convinced that the "end of the world" had come and that the "forces of the devil were at loose in the world," and that they were coming to "rape and murder my daughter." He was convinced he had to kill her to "be sure she would enter heaven without sin." After the homicide, he is convinced that the devil had "taken over my body" but that he now "must make expiation." He insists on pleading guilty to first degree murder and he will be satisfied at nothing less than a "life sentence." He received a score of 3, indicating moderately impaired functioning and a question of adequacy on this item.

A chronic paranoid schizophrenic adult male with prior prison sentences sets a fire and turns himself into the police. He states, "I can't make it on the outside. They won't admit me at the state hospital. I've got to get away for a while. I'd like to get 2 or 3 years." He received a score of 4, indicating mild incapacity and little question of adequacy on this item.

APPENDIX E: AAPL ETHICAL GUIDELINES FOR THE PRACTICE OF FORENSIC PSYCHIATRY*

I. Preamble

The American Academy of Psychiatry and the Law is dedicated to the highest standards of practice in forensic psychiatry. Recognizing the unique aspects of this practice, which is at the interface of the professions of psychiatry and the law, the Academy presents these guidelines for the ethical practice of forensic psychiatry.

Commentary. Forensic Psychiatry is a subspecialty of psychiatry, a medical specialty. Membership in the American Psychiatric Association, or its equivalent, is a prerequisite for membership in the American Academy of Psychiatry and the Law. Hence, these guidelines supplement the Annotations Especially Applicable to Psychiatry of the American Psychiatric Association to the Principles of Medical Ethics of the American Medical Association.

The American Academy of Psychiatry and the Law endorses the Definition of Forensic Psychiatry adopted by the American Board of Forensic Psychiatry:

> Forensic psychiatry is a sub-specialty of psychiatry in which scientific and clinical expertise is applied to legal issues in legal contexts embracing civil, criminal, correctional or legislative matters; forensic psychiatry should be practiced in accordance with guidelines and ethical principles enunciated by the profession of psychiatry. (Adopted, May 20, 1985)

The forensic psychiatrist practices this subspecialty at the interface of two professions, each of which is concerned with human behavior and each of which has developed its own particular institutions, procedures, values and vocabulary. As a consequence, the practice of forensic psychiatry entails inherent potentials for complications, conflicts, misunderstandings, and abuses.

In view of these concerns, the American Academy of Psychiatry and the Law provides these guidelines for the ethical practice of forensic psychiatry.

II. Confidentiality

Respect for the individual's right of privacy and the maintenance of confidentiality are major concerns of the psychiatrist performing forensic evaluations. The psychiatrist maintains confidentiality to the extent possible given the legal context. Special attention is paid to any limitations on the usual precepts of medical confidentiality. An evaluation for forensic purposes begins with notice to the evaluee of any limitations on confidentiality. Information or reports derived from the forensic evaluation are subject to the rules of confidentiality as they apply to the evaluation and any disclosure is restricted accordingly.

Commentary. The forensic situation often presents significant problems in regard to confidentiality. The psychiatrist must be aware of and alert to those issues of privacy and confidentiality presented by the particular forensic situation. Notice should be given as to any limitations.

For example, before beginning a forensic evaluation, the psychiatrist should inform the evaluee that although he is a psychiatrist, he is not the evaluee's "doctor." The psychiatrist should indicate for whom he is conducting the examination and what he will do with the information obtained as a result of the examination. There is a continuing obligation to be sensitive to the fact that although a warning has been given, there may be slippage and a treatment relationship may develop in the mind of the examinee.

The psychiatrist should take precautions to assure that none of the confidential information he receives falls into the hands of unauthorized persons.

The psychiatrist should clarify with a potentially retaining attorney whether an initial screening conversation prior to a formal agreement will interdict consultation with the opposing side if the psychiatrist decides not to accept the consultation.

In a treatment situation, whether in regard to an inpatient or to an outpatient in a parole, probation, or conditional release situation, the psychiatrist should be clear about any limitations on the usual principles of confidentiality in the treatment relationship and assure that these limitations are communicated to the patient. The psychiatrist should be familiar with the institutional policies in regard to confidentiality. Where no policy exists, the psychiatrist should clarify these matters with the institutional authorities and develop working guidelines to define his role.

III. Consent

The informed consent of the subject of a forensic evaluation is obtained when possible. Where consent is not required, notice is given to the evaluee of the nature of the evaluation. If the evaluee is not competent to give consent, substituted consent is obtained in accordance with the laws of the jurisdiction.

Commentary. Consent is one of the core values of the ethical practice of medicine and psychiatry. It reflects respect for the person, a fundamental principle in the practices of medicine, psychiatry, and forensic psychiatry. Obtaining informed consent is an expression of this respect.

It is important to appreciate that in particular situations, such as court ordered evaluations for competency to stand trial or involuntary commitment, consent is not required. In such a case, the psychiatrist should so inform the subject and explain that the evaluation is legally required and that if the subject refuses to participate in the evaluation, this fact will be included in any report or testimony.

With regard to any person charged with criminal acts, ethical considerations preclude forensic evaluation prior to access to, or availability of legal counsel. The only exception is an examination for the purpose of rendering emergency medical care and treatment.

Consent to treatment in a jail or prison or other criminal justice setting must be differentiated from consent to evaluation. The psychiatrists providing treatment in these settings should be familiar with the jurisdiction's rules in regard to the patient's right to refuse treatment.

IV. Honesty and Striving for Objectivity

The forensic psychiatrist functions as an expert within the legal process. Although he may be retained by one party to a dispute in a civil matter or the prosecution or defense in a criminal matter, he adheres to the principles of honesty and striving for objectivity. His clinical evaluation and the application of the data obtained to the legal criteria are performed in the spirit of such impartiality and objectivity. His opinion reflects this honesty and striving for objectivity.

Commentary. The adversarial nature of our Anglo-American legal process presents special hazards for the practicing forensic psychiatrist. Being retained by one side in a civil or criminal matter exposes the forensic psychiatrist to the potential for unintended bias and the danger of distortion of his opinion. It is the responsibility of the forensic psychiatrist to minimize such hazards by carrying out his responsibilities in an honest manner striving to reach objectivity.

The practicing forensic psychiatrist enhances the honesty and striving for objectivity of his work by basing his forensic opinions, his forensic reports and his forensic testimony on all the data available to him. He communicates the honesty and striving for objectivity of his work and the soundness of his clinical opinion by distinguishing, to the extent possible, between verified and unverified information as well as between clinical "facts," "inferences," and "impressions."

While it is ethical to provide consultation to an adversary in a legal dispute as a testifying or reporting expert, honesty and striving for objectivity are required. The impression that a psychiatrist in a forensic situation might distort his opinion in the service of the party which retained him is especially detrimental to the profession and must be assiduously avoided.

Honesty, objectivity and the adequacy of the clinical evaluation may be called into question when an expert opinion is offered without a personal examination. While there are authorities who would bar an expert opinion in regard to an individual who has not been personally examined, it is the position of the Academy that if, after earnest effort, it is not possible to conduct a personal examination, an opinion may be rendered on the basis of other information. However, under such circumstances, it is the responsibility of the forensic psychiatrist to assure that the statement of his opinion and any reports or testimony based on this opinion clearly indicate that there was no personal examination and that the opinion expressed is thereby limited.

In custody cases, honesty and striving for objectivity require that all parties be interviewed, if possible, before an opinion is rendered. When this is not possible, or, if for any reason not done, this fact should be clearly indicated in the forensic psychiatrist's report and testimony. Where one parent has not been seen, even after deliberate effort, it may be inappropriate to comment on that parent's fitness as a parent. Any comments on that parent's fitness should be qualified and the data for the opinion be clearly indicated.

Contingency fees, because of the problems that these create in regard to honesty and striving for objectivity, should not be accepted. On the other hand, retainer fees do not create problems in regard to honesty and striving for objectivity and, therefore, may be accepted.

A treating psychiatrist should generally avoid agreeing to be an expert witness or to perform an evaluation of his patient for legal purposes because a forensic evaluation usually requires that other people be interviewed and testimony may adversely affect the therapeutic relationship.

V. Qualifications

Expertise in the practice of forensic psychiatry is claimed only in areas of actual knowledge and skills, training and experience.

Commentary. As regards expert opinions, reports, and testimony, the expert's qualifications should be presented accurately and precisely. As a correlate of the principle that expertise may be appropriately claimed only in areas of actual knowledge, skill, training, and experience, there are areas of special expertise, such as the evaluation of children or persons of foreign cultures, or prisoners, that may require special training and expertise.

VI. Procedures for Handling Complaints of Unethical Conduct

The American Academy of Psychiatry and the Law does not adjudicate complaints of unethical conduct against members or others.

Complaints of unethical conduct against members of the Academy are referred to the attention of the appropriate committee of the American Psychiatric Association. Members of the Academy or of the public wishing assistance in this regard may consult, in confidence, the Chairperson of the Committee on Ethics of the Academy.

Commentary. It is the present policy of the American Academy of Psychiatry and the Law not to adjudicate complaints of unethical conduct against members or others.

General questions in regard to ethical practice in forensic psychiatry are welcomed by the Academy and should be submitted for consideration to the Committee on Ethics.

Should a specific complaint against a member be submitted to the Academy, it will be referred to the Chairman of the Ethics Committee. The Chairman will, in turn, direct the complainant to the member's local District Branch Ethics Committee.

The Academy, through its Committee on Ethics or in any other way suitable, will assist the local or national Committee on Ethics of the American Psychiatric Association in the adjudication of complaints of unethical conduct or in the developing of guidelines on ethical conduct as they relate to forensic psychiatric issues.

APPENDIX F: AMA OCCUPATIONAL HEALTH DISABILITY GUIDE ON MENTAL ILLNESS*

Introduction

This chapter discusses impairments due to mental disorders and touches upon behavioral impairments which might complicate any condition. Fundamental principles of impairment and disability, as well as an overview of the assessment of the whole person, are provided in Chapters 1 and 2. The reader is referred to those sections for a discussion of these issues. This chapter incorporates some of those principles as they relate to impairments and functional limitations associated with mental disorders, and it presents guidelines for assessing impairment severity. Some of the material is taken from Social Security Administration regulations ("The Listings of Mental Impairments") developed by a workgroup of experts in disability due to mental impairments. The workgroup was cosponsored by the Social Security Administration and the American Psychiatric Association.

Three principles are central to assessing mental impairment:

1. Diagnosis is among the factors to be considered in assessing the severity and possible duration of the impairment, but it is by no means the sole criterion.
2. Motivation for improvement may be a key factor in the outcome of impairment.
3. A complete assessment requires a longitudinal history of the impairment, its treatment, and attempts at rehabilitation.

Diagnosis and Impairment

The Diagnostic and Statistical Manual of Mental Disorders (DSM-III-R), is a widely accepted classification system for mental disorders. It is similar to another system, The International Classification of Diseases (ICD), also in widespread use. The criteria for mental disorders include a wide range of signs, symptoms, and

*Reprinted with permission from Mental and behavioral disorders, Chapter 14, in A. L. Engelberg (Ed.), *Guides to the evaluation of permanent impairment* (3rd ed., pp. 227–237). Chicago: American Medical Association, 1988.

impairments. Most mental disorders are characterized by one or more impairments. An individual may have a mental or behavioral impairment, however, without meeting the criteria for one of the mental disorders specified in the DSM-III-R or the ICD.

DSM-III-R calls for a multiaxial evaluation. Each of five axes refers to a different class of information. The first three constitute the official diagnostic evaluation, including the clinical syndromes and conditions that are the focus of treatment (Axis I), personality and developmental disorders (Axis II), and physical disorders and conditions that may be relevant to understanding and managing the care of the individual (Axis III). Axis IV (specifying and rating psychosocial stressors) and Axis V (rating adaptive functioning) may be particularly important for assessing severity of impairment.

Specific Impairments. In judging the degree of mental impairment, it is important to recognize that there are various types of mental disorders, each of which, like a physical disorder, has its own natural history and unique characteristics. It is apparent that some major mental disorders are chronic. The term "remission" rather than "cure" is used to indicate improvement, and remission may be intermittent, long-term, or short-term, and may occur in stages rather than all at once. The degree of impairment may vary considerably among patients, and the severity of the impairment is not necessarily related to the diagnosis. Indeed, diagnosis alone is of limited relevance to the objective assessment of psychiatric impairment because it does not permit sufficient insight into the nature of the impairment.

An episode of depression following a stressful life event, for instance, is often a short-term, self-limiting illness that may clear up when the stressful situation is relieved. Other affective disorders have their own patterns of recurrence and chronicity and often respond well to therapeutic interventions. Somatic and psychological treatment and adequate supervision are important in all affective disorders, because one outcome of partial, ineffective treatment may be suicide or attempted suicide. The schizophrenias are typically chronic disorders. Their onset can be insidious and recognized only in retrospect. Certain organic mental disorders, such as traumatic brain injury and lifelong mental retardation, are chronic. Treatment consists of minimizing the response to the pathology; for some patients, achieving only a degree of capability or habilitation may be a valid goal.

The types of mental dysfunctioning in various disorders are curiously similar, regardless of the specific diagnosis. Just as "fever" and "pain" are seen in different kinds of physical disorders, so "anxiety" and "hostility" may be observed in different kinds of mental disorders.

Evidence of Mental Impairments

The following recommendations on documentation are drawn from the "Listings of Mental Impairments" in regulations of the Social Security Administration.

The presence of a mental disorder should be documented primarily on the basis of reports from individual providers, such as psychiatrists and psychologists, and facilities such as hospitals and clinics. Adequate descriptions of functional limitations must be obtained from these or other sources, which may include programs and facilities where the individual has been observed over a considerable period of time. Longitudinal data are particularly useful.

Information from both medical and nonmedical sources may be used to obtain detailed descriptions of the individual's activities of daily living; social functioning; concentration, persistence, or pace; or ability to tolerate increased mental demands (stress). This information can be provided by programs such as community mental health centers, daycare centers, sheltered workshops, etc. It can also be provided by others, including family members, who have knowledge of the individual's function. In some cases descriptions of activities of daily living or social functioning given by individuals or treating sources may be insufficiently detailed and/or may be in conflict with the clinical picture otherwise observed or described in the examinations or reports. It is necessary to resolve any inconsistencies or gaps that may exist in order to obtain a proper understanding of the individual's functional restrictions.

An individual's level of functioning may vary considerably over time. The level of functioning at a specific time may seem relatively adequate or, conversely, rather poor. Proper evaluation of the impairment must take any variations in level of functioning into account in arriving at a determination of severity of impairment over time. Thus, it is vital to obtain evidence from relevant sources over a sufficiently long period prior to the date of evaluation in order to establish the individual's severity of impairment. This evidence should include treatment notes, hospital discharge summaries, and work evaluation or rehabilitation progress notes if these are available.

Some individuals may have attempted to work or may actually have worked during the period of time pertinent to the determination of impairment. This may have been an independent attempt at work, or it may have been in conjunction with a community mental health or other sheltered program, which may have been of either short or long duration. Information concerning the individual's behavior during any attempt to work and the circumstances surrounding termination of the work effort are particularly useful in determining the individual's ability or inability to function in a work setting. Results of work evaluations and rehabilitation programs can be significant sources of relevant data in regard to vocational and related impairments.

The results of well-standardized psychological tests such as the Wechsler Adult Intelligence Scale (WAIS), the Minnesota Multiphasic Personality Inventory (MMPI), the Rorschach, and the Thematic Apperception Test (TAT), may be useful in establishing the existence of a mental disorder. For example, the WAIS is useful in establishing mental retardation, and the MMPI, Rorschach, and TAT may provide data supporting several other diagnoses. Broad-based neuropsychological assessments using, for example, the Halstead-Reitan or the Luria-Nebraska batteries may be useful in determining brain function deficiencies, particularly in cases involving subtle findings such as may be seen in traumatic brain injury. In addition, the process of taking a standardized test requires concentration, persistence, and pace. Therefore, performance on such tests may provide useful data. Test results should, therefore, include both the objective data and a narrative description of clinical findings. Narrative reports of intellectual assessment should include a discussion of whether or not obtained IQ scores are considered valid and consistent with the individual's developmental history and degree of functional restriction.

Assessing Impairment Severity

The Social Security Administration's "Listings of Mental Impairments" suggest four areas for assessing the severity of mental impairments. Severity is assessed in terms of functional limitations on activities of daily living; social functioning; concentration, persistence and pace; and adaptive functioning in response to stressful circumstances. Independence, appropriateness, and effectiveness are all considered when assessing impairment severity. The four areas of functional limitation are discussed below:

1. *Activities of daily living* include activities such as self care and personal hygiene, communication, ambulation, attaining all normal living postures, travel, nonspecialized hand activities, sexual function, sleep, and social and recreational activities (see Glossary subsection). In the context of the individual's overall situation, the quality of these activities is judged by their independence, appropriateness, and effectiveness. It is necessary to define the extent to which the individual is capable of initiating and participating in activities independent of supervision or direction.

What is assessed is not simply the number of activities that are restricted but the overall degree of restriction or combination of restrictions. For example, a person who is able to cook and clean might still have marked restrictions of daily activities if he or she were too fearful to leave the home or neighborhood, hampering the ability to obtain treatment or even to shop.

2. *Social functioning* refers to an individual's capacity to interact appropriately and communicate effectively with other individuals. Social functioning includes the ability to get along with others, such as family members, friends, neighbors, grocery clerks, landlords, or bus drivers. Impaired social functioning may be demonstrated by a history of altercations, evictions, firings, fear of strangers, avoidance of interpersonal relationships, social isolation, etc. Strength in social functioning may be documented by an individual's ability to initiate social contacts with others, communicate clearly with others, interact and actively participate in group activities, etc. Cooperative behaviors, consideration for others, awareness of others' feelings, and social maturity also need to be considered. Social functioning in work situations may involve interactions with the public, responding appropriately to persons in authority, such as supervisors, or cooperative behaviors involving co-workers.

Again, it is not the number of areas in which social functioning is impaired, but the overall degree of interference with a particular functional area or combination of such areas of functioning. For example, a person who is highly antagonistic, uncooperative, or hostile, but is tolerated by local storekeepers may nevertheless have marked restrictions in social functioning because that behavior is not acceptable in other social contexts, such as work.

3. Concentration, persistence, and pace refer to the ability to sustain focused attention sufficiently long to permit the timely completion of tasks commonly found in work settings. In activities of daily living, concentration may be reflected in terms of ability to complete tasks in everyday household routines. Deficiencies in concentration, persistence, and pace are best observed in work and work-like settings. Major impairment in this area can often be assessed through direct psychiatric examination and/or psychological testing, although mental status examination or psychological test data alone should not be used to accurately describe concentration and sustained ability to adequately perform work-like tasks. On mental status examinations, concentration is assessed by tasks such as having the individual subtract serial sevens from 100. In psychological tests of intelligence or memory, concentration is assessed through tasks requiring short-term memory or through tasks that must be completed within established time limits. In work evaluations, concentration, persistence, and pace are assessed through such tasks as filing index cards, locating telephone numbers, or disassembling and reassembling objects. Strengths and weaknesses in areas of concentration can be discussed in terms of frequency of errors, time it takes to complete the task, and extent to which assistance is required to complete the task. A person who appears to concentrate adequately on a mental status examination or in a psychological test situation may not do so in a more "real life" work-evaluation program.

4. Deterioration or decompensation in work or work-like settings refers to repeated failure to *adapt to stressful circumstances*, which cause the individual either to withdraw from that situation or to experience exacerbation of signs and symptoms of his or her mental disorder (i.e., decompensation) with an accompanying difficulty in maintaining activities of daily living, social relationships, and/or maintaining concentration, persistence, or pace (i.e., deterioration that may include deterioration of adaptive behaviors). Stresses common to the work environment include decisions, attendance, schedules, completing tasks, interactions with supervisors, interactions with peers, etc.

Special Considerations

Particular problems are often involved in evaluating mental impairments in individuals who have long histories of repeated hospitalizations or prolonged outpatient care with supportive therapy and medication. Individuals with chronic psychotic disorders commonly have their lives structured in such a way as to minimize stress and reduce their signs and symptoms. Such individuals may be much more impaired for work than their signs and symptoms would indicate. The results of a single examination may not adequately describe these individuals' sustained ability to function. It is, therefore, vital to review pertinent information relative to the individual's condition, especially at times of increased stress.

Effects of Structured Settings. Particularly in cases involving chronic mental disorders, overt symptoms may be controlled or attenuated by psychosocial factors such as placement in a hospital, board and care facility, day treatment program, or other environment that provides similar structure. Highly structured and supportive settings may greatly reduce the mental demands placed on an individual. With lowered mental demands, overt signs and symptoms of the underlying mental disorder may be minimized. However, the individual's inability to function outside such a structured and/or supportive setting may not have changed. An evaluation of individuals whose symptoms are controlled or attenuated by psychosocial factors must consider the ability of the individual to function outside such highly structured settings.

Effects of Medication. Attention must be given to the effect of medication on the individual's signs, symptoms, and ability to function. While psychotropic medications may control certain primary manifestations of a mental disorder, such as hallucinations, such treatment may or may not affect the functional limitations imposed by the mental disorder. In cases where overt symptoms are attenuated by psychotropic medications, particular attention must be focused on the functional restrictions that may persist. These functional restrictions are also to be used as the measures of severity of impairment.

Neuroleptics, the medicines used in the treatment of some mental illnesses, may cause drowsiness, blunted affect, or other side effects involving other body systems. Such side effects must be considered in evaluating overall severity of impairment as well as the patient's functional capacity. A medication necessary to control signs and symptoms such as hallucinations may secondarily cause an "amotivational"-like syndrome.

Effects of Rehabilitation. Of paramount importance to the evaluator is the degree of vocational limitation suffered by the individual, which may range from minimal to total. The severity of an impairment may vary with the course of the illness, and when an individual is ready for discharge, vocational skills may be intact, or the individual may have slight, moderate, or severe limitations that may or may not be reversible. The evaluator must judge the possible duration of any remaining impairment, whether remission may be fast or slow, whether it might be partial or total, and whether it is likely to remain stable or get worse. Upon such considerations will depend any clinical judgment about degree of impairment.

Rehabilitation is a sine qua non in treating most patients who have recovered or are recovering from the acute phase of mental disorder, especially a major mental disorder. Even if it is not possible to effect total "remission" or "cure," the outcome may be considered worthwhile if the individual has been able to move from one degree of impairment to one of a lesser degree.

For some persons, lack of motivation seems to be a major cause for continuing impairment. Yet, with proper rehabilitative measures many patients, including some patients with organic illnesses, achieve improvement of function. Determination of permanent impairment is often imprecise, and rarely is there certainty that it exists. The use of such a determination is pessimistic, providing an adverse prediction that may well be self-fulfilling. However, the tendency for physicians and others to minimize impairment of a psychiatric nature must also be considered. Patients may not be referred for potentially helpful rehabilitation.

An important aspect of rehabilitation is the recognition that an individual on certain types of medication may be able to sustain a satisfactory degree of functioning, whereas without medication, he or she might fail to do so. For instance, there may be only a slight problem in the thinking process while the patient is taking suitable medication, but a severe one if the patient is not taking medication. Another vital part of the rehabilitation effort is to educate family and potential employers about the importance of maintenance doses of the medication, as well as about the possibility that the patient may reexperience symptoms while taking or not taking medication.

Another consideration is that an employer needs reassurance that a worker on proper medication and in the proper job is a safe worker. An example is the control of epileptic seizures with medication. Education of the patient's family, employer, and fellow workers in such matters is vital and should be a part of the rehabilitation process.

Just as there are degrees of impairment, "total rehabilitation" may not be possible. To use an example from physical medicine, it is impossible for an amputated leg to be replaced, and the affected individual cannot hope to regain perfect, preinjury ambulation. But a well-fitted prosthesis, accompanied by training in its use, can greatly improve ability to walk. If, in addition, the individual obtains suitable private or public transportation, he or she may well be totally restored to gainful employment, unless total ambulation is a requirement of the job. Even if it is, an employer could provide alternative tasks, or modify existing tasks so that they can be performed successfully by an amputee who makes skillful use of a suitable prosthesis.

Obviously, the analogy between the loss of a limb and the loss of capability resulting from a mental disorder has limitations. Nonetheless, it is important to recognize that residual impairment from a mental disorder may be just as real and severe as impairment resulting from a physical disorder or injury. The link between motivation and recovery may need strengthening in individuals impaired either by physical or mental illnesses, and this is a task for rehabilitation psychiatry. The provision by the employer of alternative tasks, or the modification of existing work conditions, may be an important part of restoration to vocational ability for a patient with mental illness, just as it is for one with a physical illness, or for one with an illness that combines elements of both.

Controversial Impairment Categories. Each of the various entitlement programs and systems of disability assessment may recognize some mental disorders and reject others as "legitimate" causes of mental impairment. There is controversy about the personality disorders (especially antisocial personality disorder) and about alcoholism and substance abuse and dependence. The adjustment disorders also present a dilemma to the evaluator. They are characterized by abnormal emotional responses to stressful life events that resolve in a short period of time when the stressor is removed. Some experts do not consider these adjustments to life circumstances as "medical impairments."

Pain. The assessment of impairment due to the perception of pain, especially in circumstances in which the complaint exceeds what is expected based on physical findings, is complex and controversial. Although this issue is discussed elsewhere in the *Guides*, it is germane to mental and behavioral disorders. The perception of pain may be distorted by mental disorders. Pain may be an element in a somatic delusion in a patient with a major depression or a psychotic disorder. It may become the object of an obsessive preoccupation or a chief complaint in a conversion disorder. The latter has been called "psychogenic pain disorder" or "idiopathic pain disorder," but these terms are often used more loosely to describe any complaint of pain that is greater than the physician expects for the "normal" patient with the same physical findings. The more specific disorders with impairments in the perception of pain are somewhat easier to evaluate than cases in which the perception of pain is said to have a "psychogenic component." Such cases require specialized assessment, perhaps using a multidisciplinary, multispecialty approach.

Motivation. The assessment of motivation is problematic, in that motivation is often difficult to distinguish from mental impairment. When is an individual who is suffering from anhedonia and lack of energy, concentration, and initiative to be considered depressed, and when is such an individual "unmotivated"? This is a complicated clinical distinction. Ultimately it is a clinical judgment, aided by a careful investigation of the history of level of effort and accomplishment prior to the onset of an alleged impairment and a search for associated signs and symptoms of common mental disorders (such as psychosis and withdrawal in schizophrenia or sleep and appetite disturbance in major depression).

The issue of motivation cannot be ignored as a connecting link between impairment and disability. For some people, poor motivation is a major cause for continuing malfunction. The underlying character of the individual may be a major factor in whether or not he or she is likely to be motivated to benefit from rehabilitation. Personality characteristics usually remain unchanged throughout adult life. However, internal events, that is, psychological reactions, can influence the course of physical and mental illness. An individual who tends to be dependent may become more dependent as the course of the illness proceeds, and one who is inclined to act out impulses may develop a constant pattern of antisocial behavior. Indeed, the pathological development of an underlying character trait may become even more pronounced and more significant than the actual illness in deterring motivation for improved functioning. Thus, the degree of disability in the social and vocational context is not necessarily the same as the degree of impairment. The loss of function may be greater or less than the impairment might warrant, and the individual's performance may fall short of, or exceed, that usually associated with the impairment. Here the complex issue of "secondary gain" arises, involving not only the amount of compensation or financial benefit that may be awarded, but also the individual's lifestyle. The individual's motivation to recover and to be self-sufficient will either diminish or enhance the quality of life, in terms of social and vocational activities. Impairment may lead to an almost total or minimal disability depending on motivational factors. Often it is difficult for an evaluator to separate impairment and motivation. The evaluator may be able to see some clues in the clinical or family history, but these are likely to be only suggestive.

When considering the total background and underlying character and value system of the individual, it must be remembered that educational levels and financial resources of family members cannot be ignored. The evaluator should assess the usefulness of family influences, and if rehabilitation efforts are to be continued, the evaluator may recommend the inclusion of the family in the endeavor.

A Method of Evaluating Psychiatric Impairment

Although there is no available empirical evidence to support any method for assigning percentage of impairment of the whole person, the following approach to quantifying mental impairment is offered as a guide. Not everyone who has a mental or behavioral disorder is totally limited or totally impaired. Many individuals have specific limitations that do not preclude all of life's activities. On the other hand, there are individuals with less than chronic, unremitting impairments who are severely limited in some areas of function. These limiting impairments must be acknowledged as a significant concern. Some disability systems choose to recognize only rather complete disability (especially for work), while others recognize and compensate partial disability.

Medically determinable impairments in thinking, affect, intelligence, perception, judgment, and behavior are assessed by direct observation, formal mental status examination, and neuropsychological testing. Translating specific impairments directly and precisely into functional limitations, however, is complex and poorly understood. For example, current research finds little relationship between psychiatric signs and symptoms (such as those found on a mental status examination) and the ability to perform competitive work. To bridge the gap between impairment and disability, the workgroup that advised the Social Security Administration on disability due to mental impairment identified the four areas of functional limitation discussed above. In a sense they are complex impairments of social functioning that may be directly related to work or other functional pursuits such as recreation, but there is no specific medical test for any one of the four categories of functional limitation. Observations made during the medical examination should be incorporated along with other relevant and important observations that go into an assessment of activities of daily living such as social functioning; concentration, persistence, and pace; and adaptive functioning.

Table 1 provides a guide for rating mental impairment in each of the four areas of functional limitation on a five-point ordinal scale, ranging from none to extreme. It might be useful to think of the following as "anchors" for each point on the scale. "None" means that there is no impairment noted in this area of function.

TABLE 1
Impairment Due to Mental and Behavioral Disorders

	AREAS OF FUNCTION	Activities of Daily Living Social Functioning Concentration Adaptation
Class 1 No impairment	No impairment noted	
Class 2 Mild impairment	Impairment levels compatible with most useful function	
Class 3 Moderate impairment	Impairment levels compatible with some but not all useful function	
Class 4 Marked impairment	Impairment levels significantly impede useful function	
Class 5 Extreme impairment	Impairment levels preclude useful function	

Note: Table format revised for this GAP report.

"Mild" implies that any impairment that is discerned is compatible with most useful function. "Moderate" means that impairments that are found are compatible with some but not all useful function. "Marked" is a level of functional impairment that significantly impedes useful function. Taken alone, a marked impairment or limitation would not completely preclude function, but together with another marked limitation it may likely preclude useful function. "Extreme" means that the impairment or limitation is not compatible with useful function. For example, extreme limitation in activities of daily living implies complete dependency on another for personal care. In the area of social functioning extreme impairment implies that the individual engages in no meaningful social contact, such as a patient in a withdrawn, catatonic state. An extreme limitation in concentration, persistence, or pace means that the individual cannot attend to conversation or any productive task at all, such as might be seen in an acute confusional state or a complete loss of short-term memory. Extreme limitations in adaptive functioning are seen in individuals who cannot tolerate any change at all in routines or in their environment, such as those who cannot function, and decompensate or deteriorate whenever schedules of events change in an otherwise structured environment. Such individuals might have a psychotic episode whenever a meal is not served on time or might have a panic attack whenever they are left without companions in any environment.

In an otherwise ordinary individual one area of extreme impairment would be likely to preclude performance of any complex task, such as recreation or work. Two or more areas of marked limitation would also be likely to preclude performance of complex tasks without special support or assistance, such as provided in a sheltered environment. An individual who was impaired to a moderate degree in all four areas of function would be significantly limited in many, but not all, complex tasks. Mild and moderate limitations reduce overall performance but do not preclude performance.

Translating these guidelines for rating individual impairment on *ordinal* scales into a method for assigning percentage impairments, as if the ratings were made on precisely measured *interval* scales, is not recommended. For example, we cannot be certain that the difference in impairment between a rating of mild and moderate is the same as the difference between moderate and marked. Furthermore, a moderate impairment does not imply 50% limitation in useful function. Similarly, a rating of moderate impairment in all four areas of function does not imply a 50% impairment of the whole person. In reality, however, physicians often are required to make such judgments. It is important to remember that such judgments are based on clinical impression rather than on empirical evidence. In those circumstances in which it is essential to make a percentage rating, the ordinal scale might be of some help: one could assume that the extreme rating approaching 100% mental impairment is similar to a coma, which is the extreme impairment of central nervous system function and level of consciousness.

Eventually research may support the direct link between medical findings and percentage of mental impairment. Until that time the medical profession must refine its concepts of mental impairment, improve its ability to measure limitations, and continue to make clinical judgments.

Example. A 27-year-old single woman is referred for evaluation for mental impairment. She has a nine year history of chronic paranoid schizophrenia. She has not worked for longer than two months at a time since dropping out of business college at the age of 19 years. The young woman has lived at home, and was cared for and supported financially by her aging parents, who recently moved to a retirement community. For the past three months she has been living in a cooperative apartment and has shown some ability to care for herself, although she needs to be reminded constantly to bathe, to take her medications, and to complete her household chores. She has little self-confidence and does not engage independently in any activities, including cooking, although when someone insists, she is capable of doing so. Once she initiates a task, she can complete it in a timely manner. She has no friends, never initiates a conversation, and when she is approached or prodded, she becomes terrified and occasionally abusive. The woman remains quite paranoid, concerned that everyone "knows my mind." Her attention span is limited to 25–30 minutes, however, and she frequently "blocks" in her speech and is unable to complete a thought. Although she has been hospitalized only twice, she frequently stops taking her neuroleptic medications, which are generally quite effective in controlling her delusions and hallucinations. Both times she was employed she became overwhelmed by the pressures of work deadlines, blamed her co-workers for slowing her down, stopped her medications, and required a return to intensive treatment. She handles some of the changes in her environment well but has considerable difficulty with the demands of time and with separation from her family.

Impairment: The evaluator concludes that her activities of daily living and social functioning are markedly impaired, and her ability to concentrate, maintain a reasonable pace, and adapt to change are, at best, moderately impaired. However, the evaluator feels that in more demanding social or vocational situations this woman would also be markedly impaired in concentration and adaptation. Therefore, he concludes that overall she is markedly impaired.

Reference

Social Security Administration. (1985). Federal old-age, survivors and disability insurance: Listing of impairments. Mental disorders; Final rule. Fed Reg 20 CFR Part 404 (Reg No 4) 50 (167), 35038-35070.

Glossary

Correct standardized usage of terminology related to the evaluation of medical impairment and disability is essential. Semantic distinctions between terms assume legal importance. This Glossary provides definitions of terms that are used in the *Guides*, and definitions of other terms related to impairment and disability evaluations that may be of interest to the reader, although they are not mentioned in the *Guides*. To assist the reader in distinguishing the evaluation of impairment from that of disability, this Glossary is in two sections: the first section contains terms related to impairment; the second section contains terms related to disability evaluation, Workers' Compensation, and employability.

Impairment

Activities of Daily Living

Activity	*Example*
Self care and personal hygiene	Urinating, defecating, brushing teeth, combing hair, bathing, dressing oneself, eating
Communication	Writing, typing, seeing, hearing, speaking

Activities of Daily Living (*continued*)

Activity	*Example*
Normal living postures	Sitting, lying down, standing
Ambulation	Walking, climbing stairs
Travel	Driving, riding, flying
Nonspecialized hand activities	Grasping, lifting, tactile discrimination
Sexual function	Having normal sexual function and participating in usual sexual activity
Sleep	Restful nocturnal sleep pattern
Social and recreational activities	Ability to participate in group activities

Apportionment: Apportionment is the determination of the degree to which each of various occupational or nonoccupational factors has contributed to a particular impairment. For each alleged factor, two criteria must be met:

(a) The alleged factor could have caused the impairment, which is a *medical* decision, and

(b) in the particular case, the factor did cause the impairment, which is a *nonmedical* determination.

Clinical Evaluation: The clinical evaluation is the collection of data by a physician for the purpose of determining the health status of an individual. The data include information obtained by history; clinical findings obtained from a physical examination; laboratory tests including radiographs, electrocardiograms, blood tests, and other special tests and diagnostic procedures; and measurements of anthropometric attributes and physiologic and psychophysiologic functions.

Disfigurement: Disfigurement is an altered or abnormal appearance. It may be an alteration of color, shape, or structure, or a combination of these. Disfigurement may be a residual of an injury or disease, or it may accompany a recurrent or chronic disorder of function or disease. It may produce either social rejection or impairment of self-image, with self-imposed isolation, alteration of lifestyle, or other changes in behavior.

Impairment: Impairment is the loss of, loss of use of, or derangement of any body part, system, or function.

Permanent impairment is impairment that has become static or well stabilized with or without medical treatment, or that is not likely to remit despite medical treatment of the impairing condition.

Evaluation or rating of impairment is an assessment of data collected during a clinical evaluation and the comparison of those data to the criteria contained in the *Guides*.

Intensity and Frequency: The intensity and the frequency of occurrence of symptoms or signs occasionally are useful in rating impairment. These can be graded as follows:

Intensity is:

(a) *minimal* when the symptoms or signs constitute an annoyance but cause no impairment in the performance of a particular activity;

(b) *slight* when the symptoms or signs can be tolerated but would cause some impairment in the performance of an activity that precipitates the symptoms or signs;

(c) *moderate* when the symptoms and signs would cause marked impairment in the performance of an activity that precipitates the symptoms or signs;

(d) *marked* when the symptoms or signs preclude any activity that precipitates the symptoms or signs.

Frequency is:

(a) *intermittent* when the symptoms or signs occur less than 25% of the time when awake;

(b) *occasional* when the symptoms or signs occur between 25% and 50% of the time when awake;

(c) *frequent* when the symptoms and signs occur between 50% and 75% of the time when awake;

(d) *constant* when symptoms and signs occur between 75% and 100% of the time when awake.

Disability, Workers' Compensation, and Employability

Aggravation and Causation: Aggravation and causation are related to the nonmedical determination that a factor that *can* cause a particular impairment in fact *did* cause the impairment (see Apportionment). In many benefit systems, causation and aggravation must be determined before entitlements are provided. In contrast to their involvement in traumatic injuries, the roles of occupational or environmental factors in causing or aggravating disorders of the various body systems often are not obvious to the lay person; thus evaluating their roles usually requires expert medical opinion. The expert's comments should include the identification of the specific environmental forces or agents and the dates and duration of their actions. An accurate chronicle of the clinical course of the disorder, with dates, times, and locations of environmental events, is helpful in the evaluation of causation and aggravation.

An aggravation, in order to have the legal impact of a causation, must be substantial and permanent, not merely speculative. Five types of aggravations are:

(a) an occupation disorder aggravated by a supervening nonoccupational disorder;

(b) an occupational disorder aggravated by a supervening other occupational condition arising out of and in the course of employment by the same employer;

(c) an occupational disorder aggravated by a supervening other industrial condition arising out of and in the course of employment by a different employer;

(d) an occupational disorder aggravated by a preexisting nonoccupational condition;

(e) an occupational disorder aggravating a preexisting nonoccupational condition.

Disability: Disability is the limiting loss or absence of the capacity of an individual to meet personal, social, or occupational demands, or to meet statutory or regulatory requirements.

Permanent disability occurs when the degree of capacity becomes static or well stabilized and is not likely to increase in spite of continuing medical or rehabilitative measures. Disability may be caused by medical impairment or by nonmedical factors.

Evaluation or rating of disability is a nonmedical assessment of the degree to which an individual does or does not have the capacity to meet personal, social, or occupational demands, or to meet statutory or regulatory requirements.

Employability: Employability is the capacity of an individual to meet the demands of a job and the conditions of employment.

Employability Determination: Employability determination is a management assessment of the individual's capacity to meet the demands of a job and the conditions of employment. The management carries out an assessment of performance capability to estimate the likelihood of performance failure and an assessment of the likelihood of future liability in case of human failure. If either likelihood is too great, then the individual will not be considered employable in a particular job.

Medical Determination Related to Employability: The medical determination of employability is a statement by a physician about the relationship of an individual's health to the demands of a specific job, such as the demands for performance, reliability, integrity, durability, and overall useful service life as defined by the employer. The physician must ensure that the medical evaluation is complete and detailed enough to obtain the clinical information needed to draw valid conclusions. The physician's tasks are: to identify impairments that could affect performance and to determine whether or not the impairments are permanent; and to identify impairments that could lead to sudden or gradual incapacitation, further impairment, transmission of a communicable disease, or other adverse conditions.

In estimating the risk factors, the physician should indicate whether or not the individual represents a greater risk to the employer than someone without the same medical condition, and indicate the limits of the physician's ability to predict the likelihood of an untoward occurrence.

Possibility and Probability: Possibility and probability are nonspecific terms without true statistical or legal meanings. They refer to the likelihood that an injury or illness was caused by a stipulated employment or other event. *Possibility* sometimes is used to imply a likelihood of less than 50%. *Probability* sometimes is used to imply a likelihood of greater than 50%.

APPENDIX G: GLOSSARY

Affidavit: A factual statement made under oath to tell the truth. By definition, an affidavit is not hearsay.

Affirmative Defense: Allegation and proof by a defendant of facts that excuse or contradict allegations of the plaintiff, for example, insanity defense, self-defense, and contributory negligence. The defendant has the burden of proof in the affirmative defense.

Amicus Curiae (Friend of the Court): This term describes an individual or organization joining existing litigation in order to contribute special knowledge to the court.

Appeal: The process by which a trial court's determinations of law are reviewed by a court with authority to find error and direct further corrective action.

Arraignment: The first court hearing before a judge in the criminal process during which time the defendant is informed officially of the charges and enters a plea.

Beyond a Reasonable Doubt: The level of factual proof required for a criminal case. It does not require certainty, but rather requires the absence of reasonable doubt.

Bill of Rights: The first ten Amendments to the U.S. Constitution which were adopted as restrictions on federal power.

Burden of Proof: The obligation in court of the moving party to demonstrate the existence of certain facts or to suffer loss of the proceeding. (see also Standard of Proof)

Case law: The Court's written opinion issued in deciding a lawsuit.

Clear and Convincing Evidence: The level of factual proof used in civil cases involving issues of personal liberty. The standard requires greater certainty than "more probable than not," but is not as demanding as "no reasonable doubt."

Common Law: Judicially declared law (case law) having its origins in England and drawing on established custom and tradition.

Competence: The legal recognition of an individual's ability to perform a task. The concept is not applied globally. Rather, it is directed at a specific category of demands, such as competence to assist counsel in preparing a defense, competence to manage financial affairs, or competence to give informed consent in legal or medical matters.

Complaint: The allegations of fact and law, by a plaintiff in a civil action, that give rise to the claim of relief from the court. The complaint is the civil analogue of the criminal indictment.

Confidentiality: The obligation of professionals not to disclose information received from a client without the client's consent. While primarily an ethical obligation, confidentiality may also be a legal duty. (see Privilege)

Consortium: The right, arising from the marriage contract, of a husband or wife to the other's love and services. Loss of consortium is a basis for compensatory damages.

Contributory Negligence: The causal contribution of an injured person to the circumstances leading to the injury. A person violating the speed limit might be found to be contributorily negligent when injured by a second negligent driver.

Crime: Misconduct that does injury to public interests rather than purely private interests. We view injury to society as separate from injuries suffered by a victim. For a crime to exist, both a criminal act (*actus reas*) and a guilty mind (*mens rea*) must be present.

Damages: Monetary award by a judge or jury to make an injured party whole (compensatory damages) or to discourage future violations of rights by the party found guilty (punitive damages). Another category of damages (special damages) includes ascertainable out-of-pocket losses experienced by the injured party.

Demurrer: A form of pleading in civil cases in which, for the purpose of argument, the defendant admits the factual allegations and asks the court to rule that the facts do not give rise to a violation of the plaintiff's legal rights. Many important new principles of law have been ruled upon through demurrers.

Deposition: A form of legal discovery in civil proceedings in which the litigants may question potential witnesses under oath to discover the testimony they are likely to present at trial. Testimony taken at a deposition may also be used to preserve evidence for a trial that might occur after the death of the deponent.

Dicta: Judicial opinion expressed in a decision but not central to the ruling of law in the case and, therefore, not binding as precedent for future decisions.

Discovery: In civil cases, methods of discovery include depositions and interrogatories. In criminal cases, the defendant may file motions seeking disclosure of evidence held by the prosecution that may be helpful to the defendant.

Due Process: The Fifth and Fourteenth Amendments to the Constitution guarantee individuals due process of law, which requires the government to be fair in the procedures governing legal matters. The Amendments further require the government to refrain from arbitrary actions in the exercise of its power.

Expert Witness: An individual permitted to present opinion in court on matters of fact that are beyond the expertise of ordinary citizens.

Fact Finder: The person or entity in court charged with making factual determinations necessary to the resolution of a lawsuit. While this function is generally left to a jury, a defendant may elect to have the judge serve as fact finder.

Factual Witness: A witness whose testimony is confined to matters that can be reported without opinion.

Fiduciary: A person, such as a trustee, with an obligation to promote the best interests of another with diligence and to refrain from any action that would further the self-interest of the fiduciary. A fiduciary relationship may arise from the superior skill and knowledge of one party to a relationship.

Guardian: Sometimes known as a conservator, the guardian acts for a person adjudged to be incompetent on matters involving personal and financial considerations. Occasionally, two guardians may be appointed, one serving as guardian of the person and the other serving as guardian of the estate.

Guardian Ad Litem: A temporary guardian, frequently a lawyer, appointed for the specific purpose of acting on behalf of a legally incompetent person during a lawsuit. A child in a custody proceeding normally will have a guardian ad litem.

Hearsay: Literally, hearsay is any written or spoken statement not made under an oath to tell the truth. Such unsworn statements are considered unreliable in court and are excluded from evidence, unless one of the exceptions to the hearsay rule is invoked. A frequently used exception is the principle that in formulating expert opinion and testimony, expert witnesses may rely on and recite from hearsay statements.

Indictment: Allegations by a prosecutor or grand jury that an individual has engaged in criminal misconduct. Sometimes referred to as an "information," an indictment is the criminal analogue to the civil complaint.

Informed Consent: Authorization given by a person who is free from coercion or undue influence, who has been given adequate information on the decision to be made, and who has the capacity to understand the information disclosed.

Interrogatories: Written questions submitted to a party in a civil case. Interrogatories are another form of discovery, designed to prevent surprise at trial and to permit each party to present the most compelling case before the fact finder.

Insanity Defense: The response of a criminal defendant requesting to be excused for misconduct on the basis of mental condition. The American Law Institute test and M'Naghten tests are the two most widely utilized insanity defense standards.

Jail: A place in which a defendant is held prior to trial and for short periods of time after conviction. (see Prison)

Jurisdiction: The scope of a specific court's authority. A court must have authority to review the legal issues (subject matter jurisdiction) and to compel the parties to respect its decision (personal jurisdiction). Further, a court's decision in a particular case sets precedent for all similar cases arising within the court's geographic boundaries (geographic jurisdiction).

Locality Rule: The requirement, in malpractice cases, that expert witness testimony on the standard of care be restricted to the standard in the defendant's community. Increasingly, courts are relaxing the locality rule to permit testimony on national standards of care.

Negligence: A failure to exercise reasonable care that leads to (or is the proximate cause of) injury when a duty of reasonable care is owed. Malpractice is negligence by a professional.

Opinion Evidence: Testimony providing opinion rather than factual observation. Opinion evidence is permitted only on matters outside the jury's understanding and only from experts competent to render opinion on the issue.

Parole: Conditional release of a defendant from prison following a period of postconviction incarceration.

Parties: A "plaintiff" initiates a civil action; the state initiates a criminal action. The responding party in either action is the "defendant." A person initiating an appeal is an "appellant;" the responding party is the "appellee."

Patient Litigation Exception: A rule that holds that a privilege is waived if the person holding the privilege introduces the subject matter of the privilege in a legal proceeding. For example, a patient cannot claim damages for emotional injuries without waiving any existing psychiatrist-patient privilege that otherwise would shield information relevant to the patient's emotional condition before or after an accident.

Pleadings: The formal, written papers filed in civil and criminal proceedings.

Preponderance of the Evidence: The level of proof required in most civil cases. The plaintiff will prevail if his or her case has the greatest weight of the evidence or can be shown to be more probable than the defendant's case.

Prison: A place where criminal defendants are incarcerated after conviction. (see Jail)

Privacy: The legal right of a patient to expect confidentiality of information. Normally, this privacy right must be created by statute.

Privilege: A rule of evidence that excludes data from a hearing or trial derived from certain socially useful relationships such as those between attorney and client, physician and patient, or clergy and confessor.

Probable Cause: The legal requirement that there be some competent evidence before a person can be detained. For a criminal arrest, some evidence must exist establishing that a crime has been committed and that the person being arrested was involved. In civil commitment, probable cause normally requires some evidence of mental illness and harmfulness. Probable cause does not mean proof; it means only that there is a rational basis to allege and retain an individual.

Probation: Conditional release of a criminal defendant immediately following conviction.

Proximate Cause: One of the four elements of a negligence claim which produced the injury without other intervening cause.

Sovereignty: The source of the inherent powers of government. Before independence, US sovereignty was vested in the King of England. Subsequently, it has been vested in the separate states.

Subpoena: A legal order commanding an individual to appear and furnish evidence at a legal proceeding.

Standard of Proof: The degree of probability to which factual assertions must be proven to allow a moving party to prevail in litigation. For example, the state must prove a criminal defendant's guilt "beyond a reasonable doubt" in order to obtain a conviction. A person's mental illness and harmfulness must be shown by "clear and convincing evidence" before involuntary hospitalization is legal. A plaintiff must demonstrate malpractice by a "preponderance of the evidence" in order to win damages in a personal injury action. (see also Burden of Proof)

Tort: A civil wrong permitting the plaintiff to recover damages for injuries suffered. "Intentional" torts include battery, defamation, and false imprisonment. Negligence is an "unintentional" tort.

Trial: The legal proceeding that determines the factual and legal questions arising from a civil complaint or criminal indictment.

Waive: To release a right. Normally, a valid waiver can occur only when the individual is informed fully as to the right being waived and the consequences of the waiver.

GAP COMMITTEES AND MEMBERSHIP

COMMITTEE ON ADOLESCENCE
Warren J. Gadpaille, Denver, CO, Chairperson
Hector R. Bird, New York, NY
Ian A. Canino, New York, NY
Michael G. Kalogerakis, New York, NY
Paulina F. Kernberg, New York, NY
Clarice J. Kestenbaum, New York, NY
Richard C. Marohn, Chicago, IL
Silvio J. Onesti, Jr., Belmont, MA

COMMITTEE ON AGING
Gene D. Cohen, Washington, D.C. Chairperson
Karen Blank, West Hartford, CT
Eric D. Caine, Rochester, NY
Charles M. Gaitz, Houston, TX
Ira R. Katz, Philadelphia, PA
Andrew F. Leuchter, Los Angeles, CA
Gabe J. Maletta, Minneapolis, MN
George H. Pollock, Chicago, IL
Kenneth M. Sakauye, New Orleans, LA
Charles A. Shamoian, Larchmont, NY
F. Conyers Thompson, Jr., Atlanta, GA

COMMITTEE ON ALCOHOLISM AND THE ADDICTIONS
Joseph Westermeyer, Minneapolis, MN, Chairperson
Margaret H. Bean-Bayog, Lexington, MA
Susan J. Blumenthal, Washington, DC
Richard J. Frances, Newark, NJ
Marc Galanter, New York, NY
Edward J. Khantzian, Haverhill, MA
Earl A. Loomis, Jr., Augusta, GA
Sheldon I. Miller, Newark, NJ
Robert B. Millman, New York, NY
Steven M. Mirin, Belmont, MA
Edgar P. Nace, Dallas, TX
Norman L. Paul, Lexington, MA
Peter Steinglass, Washington, DC
John S. Tamerin, Greenwich, CT

COMMITTEE ON CHILD PSYCHIATRY
Peter E. Tanguay, Los Angeles, CA, Chairperson
James M. Bell, Canaan, NY
Harlow Donald Dunton, New York, NY
Joseph Fischhoff, Detroit, MI
Joseph M. Green, Madison, WI
John F. McDermott, Jr., Honolulu, HI
David A. Mrazek, Denver, CO
Cynthia R. Pfeffer, White Plains, NY
John Schowalter, New Haven, CT
Theodore Shapiro, New York, NY
Leonore Terr, San Francisco, CA

COMMITTEE ON COLLEGE STUDENTS
Earle Silber, Chevy Chase, MD, Chairperson
Robert L. Arnstein, Hamden, CT
Varda Backus, La Jolla, CA
Harrison P. Eddy, New York, NY
Myron B. Liptzin, Chapel Hill, NC
Malkah Tolpin Notman, Brookline, MA
Gloria C. Onque, Pittsburgh, PA
Elizabeth Aub Reid, Cambridge, MA
Lorraine D. Siggins, New Haven, CT
Tom G. Stauffer, White Plains, NY

Committee on Cultural Psychiatry
Ezra Griffith, New Haven, CT, Chairperson
Edward Foulks, New Orleans, LA
Pedro Ruiz, Houston, TX
Ronald Wintrob, Providence, RI
Joe Yamamoto, Los Angeles, CA

Committee on the Family
Herta A. Guttman, Montreal, PQ Chairperson
W. Robert Beavers, Dallas, TX
Ellen M. Berman, Merrion, PA
Lee Combrinck-Graham, Evanston, IL
Ira D. Glick, New York, NY
Frederick Gottlieb, Los Angeles, CA
Henry U. Grunebaum, Cambridge, MA
Ann L. Price, Avon, CT
Lyman C. Wynne, Rochester, NY

Committee on Governmental Agencies
Roger Peele, Washington, DC, Chairperson
Mark Blotcky, Dallas, TX
James P. Cattell, San Diego, CA
Thomas L. Clannon, San Francisco, CA
Naomi Heller, Washington, DC
John P.D. Shemo, Charlottesville, VA
William W. Van Stone, Washington, DC

Committee on Handicaps
William H. Sack, Portland, OR, Chairperson
Norman R. Bernstein, Cambridge, MA
Meyer S. Gunther, Wilmette, IL
Betty J. Pfefferbaum, Norman, OK
William A. Sonis, Philadelphia, PA
Margaret L. Stuber, Los Angeles, CA
George Tarjan, Los Angeles, CA
Thomas G. Webster, Washington, DC
Henry H. Work, Bethesda, MD

Committee on Human Sexuality
Bertram H. Schaffner, New York, NY, Chairperson
Paul L. Adams, Galveston, TX
Johanna A. Hoffman, Scottsdale, AZ
Joan A. Lang, Galveston, TX
Stuart E. Nichols, New York, NY
Harris B. Peck, New Rochelle, NY
John P. Spiegel, Waltham, MA
Terry S. Stein, East Lansing, MI

Committee on International Relations
Vamik D. Volkan, Charlottesville, VA, Chairperson
Robert M. Dorn, El Macero, CA
John S. Kafka, Washington, DC
Otto F. Kernberg, White Plains, NY
John E. Mack, Chestnut Hill, MA
Roy W. Menninger, Topeka, KS
Peter A. Olsson, Houston, TX
Rita R. Rogers, Palos Verdes Estates, CA
Stephen B. Shanfield, San Antonio, TX

Committee on Medical Education
Stephen C. Scheiber, Deerfield, IL, Chairperson
Charles M. Culver, Hanover, NH
Steven L. Dubovsky, Denver, CO
Saul I. Harrison, Torrance, CA
David R. Hawkins, Chicago, IL
Harold I. Lief, Philadelphia, PA
Carol Nadelson, Boston, MA
Carolyn B. Robinowitz, Washington, DC
Sidney L. Werkman, Washington, DC
Veva H. Zimmerman, New York, NY

Committee on Mental Health Services
Jose Maria Santiago, Tucson, AZ, Chairperson
Mary Jane England, Roseland, NJ
Robert O. Friedel, Richmond, VA
John M. Hamilton, Columbia, MD

W. Walter Menninger, Topeka, KS
Steven S. Sharfstein, Baltimore, MD
Herzl R. Spiro, Milwaukee, WI
William L. Webb, Jr., Hartford, CT
George F. Wilson, Somerville, NJ
Jack A. Wolford, Pittsburgh, PA

COMMITTEE ON PLANNING AND MARKETING
Robert W. Gibson, Towson, MD, Chairperson
Allan Beigel, Tucson, AZ
Doyle I. Carson, Dallas, TX
Paul J. Fink, Philadelphia, PA
Robert S. Garber, Longboat Key, FL
Richard K. Goodstein, Belle Mead, NJ
Harvey L. Ruben, New Haven, CT
Melvin Sabshin, Washington, DC
Michael R. Zales, Quechee, VT

COMMITTEE ON PREVENTIVE PSYCHIATRY
Naomi Rae-Grant, London, Ont., Chairperson
Viola W. Bernard, New York, NY
Stephen Fleck, New Haven, CT
Brian J. McConville, Cincinnati, OH
David R. Offord, Hamilton, Ont.
Morton M. Silverman, Chicago, IL
Warren T. Vaughan, Jr., Portola Valley, CA
Ann Marie Wolf-Schatz, Conshohocken, PA

COMMITTEE ON PSYCHIATRY AND THE COMMUNITY
Kenneth Minkoff, Woburn, MA, Chairperson
C. Knight Aldrich, Charlottesville, VA
David G. Greenfield, Guilford, CT
H. Richard Lamb, Los Angeles, CA
John C. Nemiah, Hanover, NH
Rebecca L. Potter, Tucson, AZ
Alexander S. Rogawski, Los Angeles, CA
John J. Schwab, Louisville, KY
John A. Talbott, Baltimore, MD
Charles B. Wilkinson, Kansas City, MO

COMMITTEE ON PSYCHIATRY AND RELIGION
Richard C. Lewis, New Haven, CT, Chairperson
Keith G. Meador, Nashville, TN
Abigail R. Ostow, Belmont, MA
Sally K. Severino, White Plains, NY
Clyde R. Snyder, Fayetteville, NC
Edwin R. Wallace, IV, Augusta, GA

COMMITTEE ON PSYCHIATRY IN INDUSTRY
Barrie S. Greiff, Newton, MA, Chairperson
Peter L. Brill, Radnor, PA
Duane Q. Hagen, St. Louis, MO
R. Edward Huffman, Asheville, NC
Robert Larsen, San Francisco, CA
David E. Morrison, Palatine, IL
David B. Robbins, Chappaqua, NY
Jay B. Rohrlich, New York, NY
Clarence J. Rowe, St. Paul, MN
Jeffrey L. Speller, Cambridge, MA

COMMITTEE ON PSYCHOPATHOLOGY
David A. Adler, Boston, MA, Chairperson
Jeffrey Berlant, Summit, NJ
John P. Docherty, Nashua, NH
Robert A. Dorwart, Cambridge, MA
Robert E. Drake, Hanover, NH
James M. Ellison, Watertown, MA
Howard H. Goldman, Potomac, MD
Anthony F. Lehman, Baltimore, MD
Kathleen A. Pajer, Pittsburgh, PA
Samuel G. Siris, Glen Oaks, NY

COMMITTEE ON PUBLIC EDUCATION
Steven E. Katz, New York, NY, Chairperson
Jack W. Bonner, III, Asheville, NC
Jeffrey L. Geller, Worchester, MA
Keith H. Johansen, Dallas, TX
Elise K. Richman, Scarsdale, NY
Boris G. Rifkin, Branford, CT
Andrew E. Slaby, Summit, NJ
Robert A. Solow, Los Angeles, CA
Calvin R. Sumner, Buckhannon, WV

Richard D. Morrill, Boston, MA
Robert J. Nathan, Philadelphia, PA
Joseph D. Noshpitz, Washington, DC
Mortimer Ostow, Bronx, NY
Bernard L. Pacella, New York, NY
Herbert Pardes, New York, NY
Marvin E. Perkins, Salem, VA
David N. Ratnavale, Bethesda, MD
Richard E. Renneker, Pacific Palisades, CA
W. Donald Ross, Cincinnati, OH
Donald J. Scherl, Brooklyn, NY
Charles Shagass, Philadelphia, PA
Miles F. Shore, Boston, MA
Albert J. Silverman, Ann Arbor, MI
Benson R. Snyder, Cambridge, MA
David A. Soskis, Bala Cynwyd, PA
Jeanne Spurlock, Washington, DC
Brandt F. Steele, Denver, CO
Alan A. Stone, Cambridge, MA
Perry C. Talkington, Dallas, TX
Bryce Templeton, Philadelphia, PA
Prescott W. Thompson, Portland, OR
John A. Turner, San Francisco, CA
Gene L. Usdin, New Orleans, LA
Kenneth N. Vogtsberger, San Antonio, TX
Andrew S. Watson, Ann Arbor, MI
Joseph B. Wheelwright, Kentfield, CA
Robert L. Williams, Houston, TX
Paul Tyler Wilson, Bethesda, MD
Sherwyn M. Woods, Los Angeles, CA
Kent A. Zimmerman, Menlo Park, CA

LIFE MEMBERS

C. Knight Aldrich, Charlottesville, VA
Robert L. Arnstein, Hamden, CT
Bernard Bandler, Cambridge, MA
Walter E. Barton, Hartland, VT
Viola W. Bernard, New York, NY
Murray Bowen, Chevy Chase, MD
Henry W. Brosin, Tucson, AZ
John Donnelly, Hartford, CT
Merrill T. Eaton, Omaha, NE
O. Spurgeon English, Narberth, PA
Stephen Fleck, New Haven, CT
Jerome Frank, Baltimore, MD
Robert S. Garber, Longboat Key, FL
Robert I. Gibson, Towson, MD
Margaret M. Lawrence, Pomona, NY
Jerry M. Lewis, Dallas, TX
Harold I. Lief, Philadelphia, PA
Judd Marmor, Los Angeles, CA
Herbert C. Modlin, Topeka, KS
John C. Nemiah, Hanover, NH
Alexander S. Rogawski, Los Angeles, CA
Mabel Ross, Sun City, AZ
Julius Schreiber, Washington, DC
Robert E. Switzer, Dunn Loring, VA
George Tarjan, Los Angeles, CA
Jack A. Wolford, Pittsburgh, PA
Henry H. Work, Bethesda, MD

BOARD OF DIRECTORS

OFFICERS

President
Carolyn B. Robinowitz
Deputy Medical Director
American Psychiatric Association
1400 K Street, N.W.
Washington, DC 20005

President-Elect
Allan Beigel
30 Camino Español
Tucson, AZ 85716

Secretary
Doyle I. Carson
Timberlawn Psychiatric Hospital
P.O. Box 11288
Dallas, TX 75223

Treasurer
Charles B. Wilkinson
2055 Holmes
Kansas City, MO 64108

Board Members
Judith Gold
Harvey L. Ruben
Pedro Ruiz
John Schowalter

*deceased